20

)

C

# "Everything is broken"

*Life after Traumatic Brain Injury (TBI)*

Jessica Stevens

Published by
Filament Publishing Ltd
16, Croydon Road, Waddon, Croydon,
Surrey, CR0 4PA, United Kingdom
Telephone +44 (0)20 8688 2598
Fax +44 (0)20 7183 7186
info@filamentpublishing.com
www.filamentpublishing.com

© Jessica Stevens 2019

The right of Jessica Stevens to be identified as the author of this work
has been asserted by her in accordance with the
Designs and Copyright Act 1988.

ISBN 978-1-912635-33-7

Printed by IngramSpark

# Contents

"Everything is broken"

# Preface

---

**M**y life was transformed forever on 6th June 2015 when I suffered a traumatic brain injury (TBI) after a near-fatal car accident. I am writing this book because even if I manage to give one person a flicker of hope for the future, it'll all be worthwhile.

Although I cannot remember the exact minute details of the following events (or even remember everyone's names), I thought that this may provide some context for the reader about how much I have had to piece together from my own limited recollections. I also thought it may add some authenticity to the holes I will forever have in my memory relating to this time period. I have slowly pieced together the following events through the stories everyone else has told me, or from various medical reports.

I have tried to write everything in a chronological and concise order from the day of the accident to sitting down to write this account, but it will become clear that a lot of the following events all tend to overlap.

"Everything is broken"

# CHAPTER 1

# 6 June 2015 - The accident

"Everything is broken"

**T**he entire day of the accident has been completely wiped from my memory. As I have no recollection of the accident, I feel like I can list the following events in a clinical and almost detached way. Whilst people (especially those closest to me) will perhaps find such graphic details very upsetting, I have found that writing about them helps to alleviate any negativity I feel. It even feels like I'm not talking about myself.

My last memory is the Friday before the accident: it was my friend Liv's birthday party after work. I had specifically not had too much to drink though, as I was cat-sitting on Saturday afternoon (clearly a very important job!). My boyfriend Ryan and I were supposed to be looking after Jerry (Ryan's best friend Rich's cat); the drive there from my parents' house would have taken no longer than half an hour. The last memory I have before the accident is getting the tube home at about midnight and calling my mum Sue for a lift home from the station. From then on, everything is completely blank for several weeks.

I have been told by Mum that I had a lie-in and relaxed on Saturday morning at our family home in North-West London. It was a perfect summer's day: hot and sunny without a cloud in the sky. I had only just passed my driving test, and I'd had my car for a couple of months. My car was a black VW Polo; her number plate began with 'V', so her name was Velma (naturally). I got into my car to leave the house at

## "Everything is broken"

approximately 2.15pm. My parents' house is on a residential street which leads onto a main road. This is the road I was turning right across. As it is a blind bend, it is impossible to see any oncoming traffic there. However, the speed limit on that particular road is 30mph, so any oncoming traffic would have time to slow down enough for other vehicles. I was turning right across what I thought was a clear road. From what I had seen, it had been a clear road. As I was pulling across the road, a large estate car smashed into my driver's side door. Both vehicles were disabled immediately. The other car had collided with me so hard, it spun completely around to face the opposite direction. My driver's side airbag went off, but it still meant I had taken nearly the full impact of the smash.

Somehow, although I very nearly paid the ultimate price for this crash, it seems that luck was on my side that day. I am told that a road ambulance happened to be driving past to another call at the time, but they stopped to intervene in my accident as it looked so bad. Although my condition was extremely serious, I find it quite morbidly fascinating to think that I did not lose a single drop of blood in this crash. Despite the severe head injury, I was not bleeding at all: it was all internal.

My injuries were indeed so serious, the paramedics then immediately called the Air Ambulance. They would be able to fly me to the Royal London hospital A&E, (in Whitechapel, East London), within six minutes, rather than fighting through heavy central London traffic in a road ambulance. I am told that it took 15 minutes from the time of my accident until I was airborne. It really doesn't seem like the following events could have happened in such a short space of time.

A number of people (including the paramedics who had been driving past, paramedics from the Air Ambulance, firefighters and police) had been simultaneously working at the scene. The firefighters had cut my driver's side door off so the medics could easily get to me, and the police had closed the road. The roadside paramedics were about to move me, but the doctor on board the Air Ambulance had screamed at them to stop. She had seen that I wasn't reacting to anything anyone was saying to me. My eyes were also apparently completely glazed, which was a sign of my brain shutting down and me dying. I was then kept completely still as I was put into a medically induced coma*.

The police had checked for any ID in my purse. I can only imagine they felt sick as they realised I was on the same street that my house was on. They immediately ran to my front door, which was about two minutes away from the crash. They knocked for anyone at home; mum was still indoors, as she had stayed in specifically to watch the tennis (clearly vitally important). Mum therefore ignored the knocking. We have a shared driveway, so the police then ran to our back door to knock there. Mum therefore couldn't ignore them anymore.

> *'Does Jessica Stevens live here?'*
> *'Yes, why?'*
> *'I'm so sorry... she's been involved in a car accident...'*
> *'What do you mean!? She's only just left the house...'*
> *'It's at the end of your road...'*

My frantic mum ran to the end of our street with the police; she tells me her heart lurched when she immediately saw my driver's side door cut off and propped up against a wall at the side of the road. But by this point, I was already high above her in the Air Ambulance. Mum said she had been in complete shock trying to process the terrible scene in front of her when a random, hysterical woman at the side of the road had shouted out to her, 'She didn't look!' We found out much later on that this woman was the other driver's wife. I do find her viewpoint very interesting, as it later transpired she wasn't even in his car at the time.

The extent of my injuries, and the irreversible damage that had been done, were not fully known at the time. Mum then immediately called my dad Phil, who was out with my younger brother Matt. He drove back home in a complete panic; what kind of accident had it been if I needed the Air Ambulance?

After Dad and Matt got home, the police then immediately drove my parents to the Royal London hospital where I had been flown earlier. I am told this car was driven extremely skilfully and incredibly fast. It was only much later that the driver finally admitted to my parents that the reason they were taken to the hospital so quickly, is so they would have the chance to say goodbye to me. The collision had been so awful that my chances of survival were very slim.

## "Everything is broken"

Once my parents, and then Matt, had been taken to the hospital, all they could do was wait. Ryan had been calling and calling my mobile relentlessly, but it had continued to ring unanswered until it just went straight to voicemail. I had been using my phone as a Sat Nav to get to Rich's house; the police must have eventually found it in my car and handed it back to my dad.

Ryan then finally got through to him. Dad told him not to panic, but I'd been involved in a serious car accident. Ryan then immediately wanted to come to the hospital to be with me. Dad said he strenuously warned Ryan not to drive to the hospital like a maniac: he explained that I was in a stable condition, and that all anyone could do for now was wait for news from the doctors. Ryan then drove through heavy central London traffic to get to the Royal London hospital. It was about 6pm by the time he got there.

When Ryan eventually arrived, I was still in A&E. Ryan said he had walked in to be greeted by the sight of me hooked up to a multitude of cables and machines. He said he simply froze by my bed in complete shock as he tried to process what he was seeing in front of him. There were apparently bloodstains on the floor beneath my bed but, as I said beforehand, I didn't lose any blood at all in the crash. The blood on the floor was not mine, but Ryan said he did not know this at the time.

My Mum, Dad, Matt and Ryan were then eventually told I was being moved to ICU. Still, all they could do was sit around and wait for any further news. My mum said she had been distraught, wishing it was her instead. The doctors soon told her that the only reason I had survived is because of my age. Anyone older would have been killed by such a serious head injury.

It was about 3am by the time the doctors finally announced that I was stable for the time being. Ryan then insisted on driving my family back home before he then drove home himself. My parents had told him he should stay and just sleep in my bed, but he says he just couldn't face staying in my room without me. Ryan said he didn't ever stay in my room without me throughout the entire time of my coma.

I've asked everyone what happened on Sunday, but I think that entire period of time seems to have been a complete blur for everyone. I know I wouldn't have been able to deal with the uncertainty of my situation. I am the sort of person who wants to know the answer yesterday: I am stupidly impatient (perhaps even more so now). All everyone could do was try and support and be there for each other, as absolutely no one knew how things would pan out at all. Time seemed to both stand still and speed past simultaneously.

Sunday then rolled into Monday, which of course should have been the start of a normal working week. It had got to about 9.30am on Monday morning and no one had heard from me at work at the Financial Ombudsman Service near Canary Wharf (it's bizarre to think that the Royal London hospital is about a 10-minute drive from there). My friend Menal was in the same team as me and she knew something was wrong: I hadn't even been on WhatsApp since about 2pm on Saturday (unheard of!). She called my mobile; Dad answered and asked to speak to a manager. Menal said she handed the phone to our manager Mike and simply burst into tears. She said she knew something terrible must have happened if Dad was answering my mobile. Dad explained to Mike that I had been involved in a serious car accident, and it was so bad that no one knew what was going to happen.

A meeting was then held for my whole division at work, where everyone was told what had happened. I am told that lots of my colleagues were very upset and that many even left straight after they had heard (they apparently went straight to the pub, which I wholeheartedly endorse).

Everyone else had gradually found out through a series of awful phone calls between each other. I obviously don't know how everyone was reacting at the time, but I can only imagine that sharing and listening to such news was an absolute barrel of laughs. No one knew how, or even if, I would be able to come back from this.

"Everything is broken"

CHAPTER **2**

Injuries

"Everything is broken"

The days soon rolled into weeks after my accident, but I still lay silently comatose. All anyone could do was wait to see when, or even if, I would ever wake up.

I've spent a lot of time Googling the below terms; it's all made for a particularly grisly read. I've included a Glossary of terms at the end of the book.

My injuries:

- a "Moderate-Severe (Definite)" traumatic brain injury (as classified by the Mayo* system):
  - subdural haematoma*
  - extensive and bilateral subarachnoid haemorrhages*
  - cerebral oedema*
  - diffuse axonal injury (DAI)*
  - bifrontal cerebral contusion*
  - a stroke*

- score on the Glasgow Coma Scale (GCS)* at the scene of 7/15
- a large right sided haemopneumothorax*
- collapsed right lung
- a badly bruised/fractured right scapula
- a fractured pelvis
- polytrauma*

**"Everything is broken"**

I have several lengthy copies of medical reports which have been written about me, so I thought I'd include only the most joyous excerpts from them here.

*The hospital notes show that Miss Stevens had suffered a very severe traumatic brain injury. Her score on the GCS at the scene of the accident was 07/15, showing that there was a very significant impairment in conscious level. Early and subsequent brain imaging showed little and temporal lobe haemorrhagic contusions, extensive intracranial haemorrhage, and frontal and right temporal subarachnoid haemorrhage. There was also some subdural haemorrhage overlying the right tentorium cerebellum. This is clear evidence of both focal and diffuse brain damage. [...] I would grade the injury towards the very severe end of the spectrum. This is an injury from which significant neuropsychological and related sequelae would normally be expected.*
DR NEIL BROOKS, CLINICAL NEUROPSYCHOLOGY REPORT

The reason doctors had put me into a medically induced coma was to allow my body time to heal from my injuries as much as it possibly could. I therefore did not know anything about what was happening around me. Apparently, I had a huge black eye on my right side for the first few weeks. So not only did I look physically awful on the outside, but the doctors couldn't really predict what was happening on the inside in my brain. It is because of this awful uncertainty of the entire situation that my parents would only allow Ryan and my very best of friends, Claire, Svetlana and Jess, to visit me. I agree that visits would have been far too upsetting for everyone else (but I'm sure it wasn't exactly fun for those who were allowed to visit). Imagine if all my friends had come to visit me, and I was just lying there silently, with no knowledge they were even there at all. Or, at the absolute worst end of the spectrum, imagine if I had even died in front of them... there would have been no point in visiting at that stage anyway, as I cannot remember anything at all from that time (sorry guys...).

I am no longer interested in medical programmes now, even though I used to enjoy watching things like '24 Hours in A&E'. They are probably a little too close to the bone, especially if they feature patients being flown in by the Air Ambulance. I always wondered how the relatives of patients dealt with the constant beeping of machines, but everyone tells me you simply get used to it.

All I can do is thank my lucky stars that I somehow did not need brain surgery, as this would have involved a completely shaved head and possibly even removing part of my skull. I instead needed an intracranial pressure monitor*. This was a 'bolt' which helped to alleviate pressure from the brain, and it also meant I only had to have a very small section of hair cut by my right temple. So at least my hair was saved, even if I looked like Frankenstein's monster.

Everything was done for me by medical staff or machines while I was in the coma. I required a tracheostomy* and a catheter, and nurses would move my position in the bed to prevent bedsores. I was fed for weeks through a gastric feeding tube. I also had to wear a cooling-blanket to cool my body temperature, as I could not maintain a normal temperature myself. It's very strange to imagine being rendered so utterly helpless and useless...

It was about 18 days into the coma, and my parents, Ryan and Svetlana (my best friend since secondary school), were taking it in turns to sit with me. Then they were all suddenly ushered into a room with a doctor. I am told that apparently all this doctor said to them was, 'There is no hope of recovery for Jessica; everything is broken. She'll never talk again, she'll never work again, and she'll certainly never go home again.'

Wow...What can you even say to that? My parents told me that Sveta burst into tears and announced 'I'll never leave her'. Ryan simply sat with his head in his hands. Dad said that at the time, he had challenged the doctor and asked how he knew this. It wasn't a brain stem injury*, so why was there no hope for recovery? I'm assuming this doctor dealt with extremely bad news for most of his working day; there was nothing in my notes or behaviour to suggest I would make a recovery at all, so I do understand his medical point of view. The recovery rates for TBI are not good.

**"Everything is broken"**

Everyone had then travelled home in a complete daze. Dad says he knew he would have to tell Claire and Jess in person too, as he didn't want to break such awful news to them on the phone. Dad says he asked to see my best friend Jess, (aka my Twinny, who I lived with, and did similar courses with, at Uni), near her work to tell her face to face.

My best friend Claire (since primary and then secondary school) lives in Stoke with her wife, but she used to live with her family ten minutes down the road from my parents' house. Dad didn't want Claire to find out such bleak news on the phone either, so he told Claire's mum Jo what the prognosis was. Jo then waited for Claire to get the train to London to visit me before again breaking the news face to face.

Now my family, Ryan, Sveta, Jess, and Claire all knew. This whole situation was undeniably heading towards the most miserable of endings.

*Miss Stevens was weaned off sedation 2-3 weeks post-accident, but failed to wake up, and the treating team informed her family that her prognosis was poor and that she might never do so.*
DR OLIVER J FOSTER, MEDICO-LEGAL REPORT

https://www.headway.org.uk/about-brain-injury/
further-information/statistics/

# CHAPTER 3

# Waking up

"Everything is broken"

After hearing such a grim prediction of how I would be post-accident, I would have expected people to give up. However, not a single person did: my family, my best friends, and my partner all remained strong for me. Not one person stopped their visits or let their will for me to wake up diminish. Though the doctor they saw said there was no way I'd ever go home, my parents were already planning on renovating their house, so I could have the lounge as my bedroom and be taken onto the garden patio in a wheelchair in nice weather.

Doctors had then slowly begun 'weaning' me off sedation. I assume this is so I would get to some sort of state whereby I didn't need as much medical help from machines, but I'm not really sure. Dad says there was a moment where I received an anticoagulant* in my stomach and I winced in pain. Dad said that was the first time in weeks I had actually reacted to pain. Apparently, there were some points during this 'weaning' period where I had my eyes open, which I can only imagine was very unnerving for everyone around me.

I find it very touching that everyone tells me the nurses always spoke to me as if I were awake, even though I was comatose for over a month. The nurses would apparently always tell me the medical procedure they were about to perform, or some would even ask me how I was (despite the fact their questions would always be rhetorical).

## "Everything is broken"

Then one day, I was suddenly conscious. It was that quick. It is a very bizarre feeling to have 6th June 2015 – 11th August 2015 completely erased from my memory, but I suppose I don't really want to recall anything from that time period anyway. I've tried keep the following events in a tangible or sensible order, but I suppose it's more authentic to leave it confused and jumbled as all the early events are to me. I can't even really remember what I felt like when I woke up, either mentally or physically. I think I was just feeling incredibly stiff and creaky after I'd been lying down for such a long time, and I suppose I was just a bit nonplussed waking up in a medical environment I knew nothing about. It's hard to grasp onto a solid memory throughout the fog of just waking up after such a long time.

My memories go straight from getting the tube home on Friday night, to six weeks later waking up in a hospital bed. There is simply a chasm of absolute nothingness between those two moments in time for me. Even reading that back feels quite odd, but my mind is completely blank between the above two dates: it can't even be described as experiencing white noise. That time was simply a vast, blank nothingness. I personally think this is the brain's way of protecting me. I think to clearly remember such an awful car accident, and then the following events, could be very harmful (and perhaps even traumatising). Apparently, the drugs doctors had been using to knock me out were strong enough to knock out a horse, but they needed to be this strong so my body and brain could "heal" as much as possible.

The very first solid memory I can grasp onto is seeing my Mum, Nan and my Uncle Michael's girlfriend Paola walking towards my hospital bed. I simply said hi to them all as if nothing had ever happened. Even though I can remember that moment and I knew exactly who everyone was, I do not remember ever feeling scared or confused about why I was in hospital. People had printed lots of pictures to stick around my bed, and there was no one I didn't recognise or remember. I can only imagine it must've been very bizarre for everyone to have to deal with me suddenly (and casually) starting a conversation, as if nothing had ever happened, after being silent for over a month. I must've initially been told by nurses about what had happened to me, but I do not actually remember any of it at all.

Of course, my family then also explained to me that I had been involved in a very serious car accident and that I had spent the next six weeks out cold. Not really sure how I had reacted to this at the time... That same evening, I then saw my Dad (his work had given him as much time off as he wanted throughout the whole time I was unconscious). It seems odd to say that this was the first time I had spoken to any of my family members in over a month, when they'd all been a couple of feet away from my hospital bed for hours on end. Again, Dad reiterated that the accident was not my fault. I do not really remember, (or perhaps I didn't even really understand), Dad telling me that he and Mum had hired a lawyer to deal with my case. Dad said that at a time of utter horror and confusion, all they could do was focus on getting me justice and any help I needed if, (they probably thought 'when'), I woke up. The other driver ruined my life, so Dad said he wanted to make sure his own life was ruined too. My lawyer is called Kim Smerdon and she works for Boyes Turner. They are a law firm who are affiliated with Headway, the brain injury charity my parents had called for support. Throughout my recovery, Kim has been a great help to both me and my family; I will go into further detail about Boyes Turner later on in the book.

I also had my first conversation with Ryan that day; he had definitely proved how stoic he was throughout those 6 weeks. I suppose it's a good thing Ryan has a sense of humour, especially after this particular moment. He said I had told a nurse he was my boyfriend... when the nurse asked me what his name was, I apparently looked at him and said, 'Err... what is your name?' I have no recollection of this, but I guess it's good to see I was so appreciative of the hours Ryan spent sitting at my bedside...

*'Suit the action to the word, the word to the action'*

SHAKESPEARE, HAMLET *ACT III, SC I*

As I mentioned beforehand, I had only just passed my driving test so I was a very new driver: was the accident due to my own inexperience? I remember from that point onwards that it has always been reiterated to me that the accident was not my fault: it was the other driver's reckless speeding that caused it.

## "Everything is broken"

Injury-wise, I can't even remember when I was told (or who even told me) I'd suffered from a traumatic brain injury (TBI). I'm not really sure if I understood this at that point in time; perhaps I wasn't even capable of truly understanding what it meant at all. Reading 'TBI' back now however is very chilling; the brain controls everything we do, and I believe it is the very essence of who we are. I find it fascinating that everyone's brain is unique; everyone has different thought processes and opinions about absolutely everything. It is also once I've sat down to write this account that I've thought about how a TBI is simultaneously a physical injury, but also an intangible one. Yes, X-rays would show bruising to my brain, but they would reveal nothing about the damage caused to intangible things like my memory or emotions.

I suppose is only after my accident that I've started to truly consider life as an entity. I'm not religious, and I still don't know what happens to us when we die. I do, however, think we have a soul, at least of some sorts. It's hard to put into words, but I believe that, whether we have a soul or not, your whole sense of self is found in the brain. But now mine had been so badly damaged, how would I ever get back to who I was before? I still felt like me so surely, I was still thinking like me? I suppose I had no way of knowing. I didn't feel like everyone around me had changed either... but was this my brain just telling me everything was fine? Was everything actually completely backwards? Trying to process whether or not a TBI is truly just a physical injury still confuses me even now...

So, I suppose a TBI might've been enough to be getting along with, but there was more. After I'd woken up, I was also told I'd suffered from a broken pelvis, which had at least already healed when I was in the coma. I had either a broken or severely bruised my right shoulder; medical reports always disagree about this particular injury, so I don't know if it was actually broken or not. Even though I had sustained such serious injuries, I think it almost sounds like I'm trying to put on a brave face, or even lying, when I say that nothing related to the actual car accident ever actually hurt me. The only things that ever caused me any pain were the anticoagulants (which were agony, and I always hoped the nurses would forget about them... they did not).

I had very unsteady walking. I needed help walking to and from the toilet, and I required a wheelchair for anything further than that. I also had weakness in my whole body, especially down my whole right-hand side. My speech was a lot slower and I kept slurring and stammering. These were after-effects of the stroke I'd had at the time of the crash. Finally, my right arm was 'locked' bent and wouldn't straighten out at all. I was likewise very disorientated about all dates; it was 6th June yesterday, so how could it suddenly be August today? Although this definitely cannot be classed as any sort of injury, all of my jewellery had also been removed by the medical team in hospital when I was first admitted. I have six piercings in my ears, so the newest top ones had started to close up. I know it might seem like a trivial thing to complain about, but I still made my mum hunt in my jewellery box at home for more studs to bring in; although it was an unpleasant feeling, I then forced a stud back into each piercing hole. I just hope I wasn't wearing anything particularly ornate the day of the accident, as I'll never even be able to remember what it looked like, to replace it. The same could be said for the clothes I had on, as they're all long gone now (I just hope I had a nice pair of knickers on…).

It's very bizarre that it's only once I've sat down to write this account that I've realised how many things I've forgotten about. My mobile is usually never far from my hand, but it had been off and unusable since Dad had told my work about my accident the Monday after it. Just so I could at least try to have some contact with the outside world, I'd been making do with a terrible pay-as-you go phone Dad had bought for me. I have no idea how Ryan did this, but he somehow managed to save my iPhone and everything on it (all my contacts, my messages, photos…). I think my family had previously tried using my thumb to unlock it, but it wouldn't work. Now I was awake, my family gave my phone back to me, so I could at least text people from my usual number.

I was admittedly never a large person anyway, but I had still managed to lose so much weight as I had been fed through a tube for weeks. I do remember there were no mirrors anywhere, so at least I couldn't focus and obsess over how bad I looked. This was probably for the best, as my hair also looked so awful. At least Jess had put it in a French plait, and drenched it in leave-in conditioner, to try her best to save it for me. I whinged at mum to at least leave me a little handheld mirror, which she did (if only to stop my complaining). I then even started wearing foundation, and the lipstick my friends always knew that I wore: my Barry M colour-change lipstick (it's bright green, so people always give me funny looks as I apply it… but I promise it changes to pink once it's on!).

My parents, my nan and Ryan visited me every single day when I was in hospital. My Uncle Michael and Paola also came to see me whenever they could. Jess, Sveta and Claire likewise came whenever they could. It's only now that I can fully comprehend what it must have been like for my friends, and I can fully appreciate the depths of their friendship. (Jess says the moment I told her I couldn't find my 'platypus feet', aka my slippers, still makes her laugh now!) My parents had now also allowed a number of my other close friends to visit me at this stage too. Visits from everyone definitely gave me the huge amounts of encouragement and support I needed.

My parents had read up huge amounts of information on TBI, and every article had seemed to advise not allowing the person to become too fixated on an issue. Possibly as a means of distraction, I remember my parents telling me about their cats. We have a family cat called Chloe, who must be getting on for 17 now. My parents had also recently adopted another new kitten a few weeks before. I then immediately told them I would've gone into a coma years ago if it meant waking up to a new cat. They named her 'Munchie'. Not a name I would've chosen myself, but I guess 'comatosers can't be choosers'…

It's very odd how the brain works. I remember that the woman opposite me had ducklings living under her bed. I say I 'remember' this, but it obviously did not happen. That moment will always remain a memory to me however, as I really did think this woman was some sort of 'Fly Away Home' tribute act… I also initially believed that a 'pelican had saved me', which I can only assume might've been some sort of unconscious memory of comparing being in the London Air Ambulance to a mother pelican carrying her ducklings in her beak… My dad is an avid birdwatcher, so his ornithological obsession must have unconsciously worn off on me.

Another 'memory' I have is that we were all in bunk beds in the ward. I remember shushing someone visiting me, because I didn't want the person in the 'bunk' underneath me to hear. All my language was jumbled up too; I told a nurse my favourite flavour of yoghurt was horse. Even this isn't something I remember, as I thought I had actually said that my favourite colour was horse. Mum and Dad have had a lot of fun correcting all the 'memories' I've randomly created. My favourite animal is a horse, my favourite colour is pink and my favourite yoghurt flavour is strawberry, so literally everything had been completely mixed up in my brain. Dad describes it as though every idea/feeling/emotion I had was a square from a Scrabble board; everything was then jumbled around together as if in a letter tile bag and then regurgitated in a nonsensical order (which I suppose explains my 'platypus feet'!).

My speech was a lot slower and slurred due to the stroke I'd had at the time of the accident. I also kept repeating myself, as I'd instantly forget anything I'd already told people. No one told me I was repeating myself at the time; they all just humoured me and acted like it was the first time they'd heard what I was telling them. Sorry for boring you all...

To this day, I am very conscious of the ugly purple scar on my throat from the tracheostomy I had. Everyone says it's barely noticeable and I'm worrying about nothing. (I still use Bio Oil and Sudocrem on it, which seems to have calmed it down a lot.) My right arm still doesn't 100% straighten, but it's much better than how it was when I first woke up. It used to be permanently bent: I could not straighten it at all due to the stroke I had had. I was initially very upset that none of the doctors or nurses had simply straightened it; I'd been asleep for 6 weeks, you'd think someone would've had time! But then people explained that they simply couldn't stretch it out straight. It was locked into a permanently frozen, spasmodic position. Many times, I have wished I had broken my arm instead. A broken arm would've healed in a matter of weeks.

No one likes the chemical kind of medicinal stench every hospital has, and I am no exception. The lights in the ward were switched on 24/7, so I never got a proper night's rest. The nurses must've been pleased with my progress though, as they agreed to let me go home for the weekends. They made me promise I would use a wheelchair

## "Everything is broken"

at all times if I went out, and I could only have a bath using a bath-board. Although I kept my promise and used the wheelchair wherever necessary, I did not even own a bath-board; I just sat down in the shower instead. It was refreshing to be able to shower alone, as the nurses wouldn't even let me go to the toilet on my own in the hospital. I say 'wouldn't', but I guess the correct word is 'couldn't', as I could've fallen over on the way there. I was also banned from showering alone, so there was no such thing as privacy on the ward.

The first weekend I was allowed home, Ryan stayed over and I slept for about 13 hours straight; I hadn't slept in my own bed for over 6 weeks. The bag of stuff I'd had with me on the day of my accident was on my bed. My parents said that when the police gave this back to them, they had just put it straight in my room and been unable to go through it. It was quite eerie unpacking it all as if it were some sort of time capsule. I remember sadly looking at the pink pyjamas I was going to wear on Saturday night, and the outfit I was supposed to wear home on Sunday afternoon.

I went to the opticians with my parents that first weekend I was allowed home. I had asked Mum to bring me my glasses into the hospital from home, but she couldn't find them anywhere. I then asked her to bring in some of my contacts (they are the soft daily ones), but they were not strong enough for me anymore. The opticians found that my right eye had now deteriorated to the same weakness as my left eye. As I couldn't find my original glasses, I bought a completely new pair. Then of course I then found my original pair about a month later hidden in my room; I then replaced the lenses in them too. Doctors and optometrists do not know exactly why my eyesight has got worse. I was hopeful it might to back to how it was before, but it seems to have continually deteriorated (but it's hard to tell if my eyesight wouldn't have got worse with age anyway). I was always short-sighted, so now I'm just a bit blinder. I was then allowed to go home every weekend from that point; I would spend all week in a hospital bed waiting for the relief of getting to go back to my own bed for just two nights.

After living together at uni, Jess knew how I liked to always look my best. The nurses had taken my nail varnish off when I was first admitted to A&E; this is so they could monitor the oxygen levels in my blood with a pulse oximeter. Jess had offered to paint them again, but the nurses wouldn't allow it (as nail varnish would block checking the blood's oxygen levels through my fingernails). Although the nail varnish was removed from my fingernails, it had been left on my toenails. I think it is only once you cannot do things for yourself, you truly realise how many little, seemingly insignificant, things you do of your own accord without ever even really acknowledging it as a task. My toenails had got so overgrown by this point, I had to go to a local chiropodist to have them professionally cut. (I just read that back and I feel like it's the grimmest sentence I've ever written...) One day a few weekends later, Jess also met me in a coffee shop to paint my fingernails for me... at least that sounds a tiny bit more glamorous!

All of these events have a dreamlike quality in my memory. Although I was allowed to go home on Fridays for the whole weekend after my parents picked me up, I spent the remaining five days of the week in the hospital ward. Apart from that tiny bit that'd been cut short, the rest of my hair had become disgustingly knotted and tangled while I was writhing and thrashing about in my sleep. It got so bad that the nurses had wanted to cut it short. My parents had (correctly) not allowed them to. The plait Jess had put it in unfortunately did not completely save it from knotting itself into some sort of horrendous dreadlock.

Ryan had also insisted my hair wasn't cut: both he and my parents knew the repercussions they would face if (*when* they probably thought) I woke up. Ryan asked his mum Karen to come in to help with the mega de-tangling process. Armed with numerous hair oils and brushes, Karen came to visit me and she painstakingly brushed my hair for me. They would take it in turns to brush it for hours on end, trying their best to loosen the one massive dreadlock/tangle it had knotted itself into. After several conscientious hours, my hair was finally free from tangles. I don't think I'll ever be able to express my gratitude I feel towards Karen and Ryan for saving my hair. I know it might seem like a minor thing, especially when it is compared to everything else I faced in the grand scheme of things, but it meant so much to me. Karen also helped with 'Veeting' my legs (nearly two months of nothing was not a pretty sight!). I couldn't shave them due to being on anticoagulants for so long: even if I only suffered a little shaving cut, I simply wouldn't stop bleeding. My time in hospital was definitely a very glamorous affair.

## "Everything is broken"

Sticking with the topic of my appearance, I had let my roots get ridiculously bad just before the accident (my hair is naturally dark chocolate brown, but I have dyed it blonde for years). I didn't care though, because I had deliberately left them to specifically have dyed just before my upcoming holiday to Greece with Ryan. (On a side-note, if anyone is ever thinking about skipping travel insurance for a holiday, please don't. Ryan and I had to cancel our entire trip, but we didn't lose out on anything we'd already paid for, because we were insured.) So, even though it was already in dire need of being coloured anyway, my hair then had to cope with another six-plus weeks of no dye. This meant my dark roots were now nearly to my ears: now it was de-tangled, I needed it dyed too. Jess and a nurse were allowed to chaperone me to a hospital hairdresser. Jess sat with me for hours while I had my roots redone and I was finally blonde all over once again.

I think is from that moment onwards (which was no longer than a couple of weeks, or maybe even days, after I woke up) that the doctors and nurses started implementing the initial stages of the rehabilitation process. I think they must've thought if I was well enough to focus on something as vain as getting my hair done, I was definitely well enough to do something useful like walking again...

# CHAPTER 4

# Rehab – Central Middlesex

"Everything is broken"

A lthough I cannot pinpoint the exact dates I started NHS rehab in Central Middlesex, I do know that it definitely put me on the right track to recovery. I was the youngest person on my ward of about eight people, and I wanted to get out of there as quickly as I could.

Until the day I woke up, I hadn't been out of my bed in over 6 weeks, so my muscles had all massively deteriorated through lack of use (this is known as atrophy*). I wasn't allowed to shower or even go to the toilet on my own; I always had to always call a nurse for help as my walking was that bad. Not wanting to sound clichéd, but it was only when I needed help with absolutely everything that I realised how much I had taken for granted. I remember always asking the nurses to turn away, as there is nothing more off-putting than trying to have a wee as someone stares at you...

The physical damage from the accident had all occurred on my right side, as the other driver had hit the driver's side of my car. My right arm was 'locked' bent, unable to fully straighten out; my right scapula also 'winged' out, which meant it did not sit flat to my back like my left side. I couldn't even do my bra up behind my back: I had to do it up in front of me and then spin it around my back. A nurse showed me this trick, and she also helped me practise showering again. I had to sit down on a plastic seat which folded out from the wall for the majority of my showers. Having a full conversation with someone

## "Everything is broken"

whilst you're completely naked and trying to lather up shower gel is an odd feeling at first, but you just get used to it. I suppose nurses have seen it all before. This is the least glamorous thing I've ever said (since the toenails incident anyway), but I also remember another nurse shaving my armpits for me. I didn't even realise how bad they were until I had screamed in horror after Dad made a joke about them just after I had woken up; 6 weeks of unshaved pit was not a pretty sight. The nurse who helped me must've taken pity on me (or been unable to stomach my complaining), as I could not move my arms enough to do it myself. That evening, she completed this delightful procedure for me with soap, a razor and a bucket of water. It was done either extremely carefully, or after the effects of the anticoagulants had worn off; the nurse at least drew the curtains around my bed to protect the miniscule amount of dignity I had remaining.

I started seeing two muscular-skeletal physiotherapists one-on-one not long after I woke up. These physios helped me with everything from a physical perspective. They made several plaster casts for my right arm, which were gradually made straighter as the weeks went by. I had to wear a cast for up to six hours during the day to encourage the muscles to stretch and straighten back out into a 'normal' shape again. I couldn't get these casts wet, so I didn't wear them when showering. I am glad I didn't have to wear one all the time, as I would never have been able to sleep with one on.

I remember one day the physios took me out in my wheelchair to the ASDA around the corner from the hospital. I was allowed to buy new pyjamas, and things like trainers and casual wear. Although I was happy with this trip out into the fresh air, it was only much later on that I realised this was actually a test to see how well I coped in large surroundings with lots of people, and to see how well I coped with handling money. I have discovered that many brain damaged people go bankrupt within a year of discharge from hospital, as handling money suddenly becomes an impossible or abstract task for the injured brain to deal with. Many also have to re-learn about the potential dangers of seemingly everyday things (e.g. the concept of sustaining burns from the boiling water of a kettle).

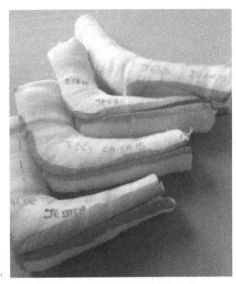

The casts for my right arm getting gradually straighter as I progressed.

The physiotherapists also helped me with what I presumed at the time were just everyday, mundane things that everyone can do. One worksheet I as given included naming exotic animals (e.g. a lion); this was testing what I recognised or remembered. I've always loved animals and I was happy I still knew what everything on the sheet was. However, the second part of the worksheet involved joining letters to numbers, in alternating alphabetical to numerical order (e.g. 1 - A – 2 - B and so on). My brain could not cope with that at all, and I gave up at the letter C! Next, I had to draw a clock. Everyone knows you draw the 12, 3, 6 and 9 points in first before filling the other numbers in a circle. Though I did include all of the right numbers 1-12, my clock looked very squashed and haphazard. I then had to draw the hands on at a specific time; though it again didn't look very neat, I did remember the big hand meant minute and the little hand meant hour. Finally, I had to draw a cube (which I think was a way of measuring my abstract thinking). I know I missed out a whole bottom line of this cube, but I remember thinking I'd drawn it totally correctly.

Although it was hardly ideal to have weakness in my entire dominant side (hemiparesis)*, in some ways I suppose it forced me into completing rehabilitation to the best of my abilities. If it had been my

## "Everything is broken"

left side affected, I honestly don't know how I would have dealt with this. I assume I would've been incredibly lazy and not really bothered with it; why should I care about my non-dominant side anyway? But I suppose that's just another 'what if' that I don't really want to waste time thinking about. I had to learn how to do everything again. Or maybe 'learn' is the wrong word, as I still knew how to write all of the letters of the alphabet. Miraculously, I had not forgotten anything or anyone I had already known beforehand. Perhaps it's better to say I had to practise everything again. Whereas once my handwriting was very neat, I don't think it'll ever go back to the way it was before the accident. Although it has improved over time, my hand still gets stupidly tired if I have to write anything longer than a birthday card. My speed is also greatly affected, whereas once upon a time I could write lecture notes for an hour. I was given this exercise to practise hand movements, which helped increase my dexterity:

### Hand exercises
1. Top of thumb to top of finger - repeat on all fingers
2. Thumb to base of finger - repeat on all fingers
3. Thumb to base of finger, then slide up - repeat on all fingers
4. Drumming fingers - lift wrist up then place fingers down then up
5. Turn 1kg weight in hand

I went to the special rehab room in the hospital once a week to practice physical activity. One thing I did was jump on a miniature trampoline whilst holding onto a rail; I found this very nerve-wracking and I could only jump up a couple of inches at a time.

I remember one day there wasn't a nurse free to help me shower in the morning before I went along to this rehab room. As I've already said, I'm very short sighted, but this didn't really matter sitting in a hospital be all day: what did I even need to see? A nurse came along to take me to the room, so I didn't bother even putting my glasses on. I wasn't allowed to walk that far, so the nurse took me along in a wheelchair. She wheeled me into the room and left; another nurse said she'd see me in 2 minutes. I then heard 'Jessica?!' from the other side of the room. Un-showered and un-bespectacled, I squinted around in dread. It was only as he approached me and gave me a massive hug that I realised it was a guy called Yaron, whom I hadn't seen for years. He had been in my form back at school, and he also lived in my parents' street. Yaron was working as a physiotherapist at Central Middlesex; whoever said London is a big place is very wrong. It is a village where you can't go anywhere without seeing someone you know!

The nurses encouraged me to try and walk unaided, and I also practiced walking rather than using my wheelchair when I went home. Soon my arm (though still not 100% straight) was almost looking normal, and I don't think anyone would've even noticed the differences between my right and left arms if I hadn't shown them.

I was officially discharged from Central Middlesex on 4th September 2015. I had had to take a wheelchair every time I was allowed to stay at home at the weekends, but now I left walking unaided. I was allowed to spend one weekend at home before I was then admitted to another hospital.

"Everything is broken"

# CHAPTER 5

# Rehab – Edgware Community Hospital (NRC)

"Everything is broken"

started live-in rehab at the Royal Free Neurological Rehabilitation Centre (NRC) at Edgware Community Hospital on 7th September 2015. I remember it had lots of long winding corridors, and I always got lost on the way to the food hall or toilets; as it is only about a 10-minute drive from my parents' house, I was still allowed to go home at the weekends. My family visited every day (they definitely had no excuse now, as Central Middlesex had been miles away!) and lots of my friends came to see me too. At least I also had my own large room here, so it was a relief to have a bit of privacy rather than being stuck on a ward of beds and eyes. I was allowed to shower alone (hooray!) and I was even standing up in the shower by this point too (even bigger hooray!).

I was given a timetable of my daily activities; each day involved working on different aspects of my recovery with a different medical professional. Most of the work I did at NRC was paper-based; I've always been a bit of a neat-freak, and now I'm annoyed with myself that I recycled most of it after I was discharged. But I did find some paperwork filed away, most of this section will have to rely on my very hazy memories (or complete lack thereof)…

One printed report I found was from the vocational occupational therapist I saw, who was called Sarah. She had an assistant called Heidi, whom I would often work with too. Sarah organised all the different strands of support I needed with each different issue, and she was very diligent. She had worked with HR at my work to create a 'return to work' plan, which would focus on managing any potential fatigue, my commute, my workstation, and a graded return back into full time hours.

I also started my period on the same day I moved into my room here. I hadn't seen it for a while, so I guess I was glad it had come back (even if it was at such an inopportune moment!). I would like to have kids in the future, so it was good to see that at least everything seemed to be working biologically.

It is only once I actually sat down to collect facts to write this account that I realised that apart from the anticoagulants, I hadn't taken any medication at all since the day I woke up. I guess the anticoagulants weren't even medication really, they just related to lack of movement, so anyone in my position would've needed them. Mum says I was on a ridiculous amount of medication for absolutely everything when I was in the coma; my parents had been very worried as they wondered how, or even if, I would ever be weaned off everything. Turns out I just apparently enjoy causing unnecessary worry...

Again, I had help here from another muscular-skeletal physiotherapist. Although this was not the specific kind of physio I needed, it still helped to drastically improve my movements and walking. It is only through getting up and walking around that my walking ability actually improved. (I hadn't really believed in the mantra 'use it or lose it' before, but I guess I'm the literal walking proof of this now...) I'm not sure if people are just trying not to hurt my feelings, but everyone says there is nothing wrong with my walking now, and my gait appears completely fine, whereas beforehand, I think I did suffer with ataxia*. I guess either way, any kind of walking was a massive improvement compared to barely being able cross a corridor in Central Midd.

I was very conscious about my speech being slurred and difficult to understand, so I started seeing a speech therapist. She gave me lots of speech exercises to practice both in the sessions and on my own. This definitely helped (even if talking to myself did make me feel a bit ridiculous). I think now I only forget words or stutter when I am extremely tired, or when I'm trying to simultaneously think about lots of different things.

The food at the NRC wasn't spectacular. Whereas before in Central Midd, we all ate our meals off a tray in our beds, here there was a designated meal hall where everyone could sit and eat together if they wanted to. Most days I did this. One nurse asked if I wanted to make my own breakfast in the mornings, so she would come to wake me up before I went to the kitchen with her to take charge of at least one of my own meals (even if it only involved a cup of coffee and putting milk on a bowl of cereal). Making meals would obviously be a vital part of anyone's life once they were out of the rehab situation. Everything in the patients' kitchen was labelled (e.g. my spoon would be in the drawer labelled 'cutlery'); the nurses would always be watching to see if an injured brain could comprehend this.

The NRC was so close to our parents' houses, I remember Sveta came to see me after work with gnocchi she'd cooked for me. I got to eat home-cooked meals at the weekend, but this was easily the best meal I'd had on a weekday. (I just hope I never have to return the favour for Sveta, as my cooking is shockingly bad.)

I am incredibly grateful for all the medical help I received at the NRC. However, I have to be honest and say whilst I participated with every effort at the time, I cannot remember every detail about it. In fact, it is only once I have sat down to write this account that I realise how little I remember of that time. I can only seem to recall completely random events. For example, I distinctly remember doing a very random test with one of the inpatient occupational therapists, Jackie. I'm not even sure if this test has a name, but we'll call it the peg test; using my right hand, I had to clip several pegs onto a surface, before unpegging them again as quickly as I could. This was to help improve my coordination on my dominant side; it also helped my dexterity and the 'stiffness' which had built up on this side.

Added to my hair dramas, another event that clearly stands out in my mind also involves my looks. I remember Jackie asked if I wanted to do anything that would help me in 'normal' everyday life. I immediately said I wanted to practise applying my makeup; the last day I had worn

## "Everything is broken"

a full face had been the day of my accident. Jackie agreed, so I brought in my makeup bag (and makeup remover for any accidents). I practised it again very slowly, as my right arm was still very wobbly. Occupational Therapy is supposed to centre around getting back to doing things that are important to you: wearing makeup has always been a part of me, so I was very happy that I was able to do girly stuff again.

I was concerned I would come across as a bit egocentric if I admitted to wanting to practise my makeup, especially when paired with my need for my hair to be sorted out. As much as some people think my appearance should've been the last thing on my mind, how I looked still mattered personally to me. Everything, especially after a life-changing accident, depends on your own personal perspective. Though it meant everything to me, having dyed hair or the ability to apply eyeliner may mean absolutely nothing to somebody else.

On 6th October 2015, after I'd been at the NRC for a month, my friend Leesa, who lived one street away from me at the time, came to visit me as a surprise. I hadn't actually seen Leesa since we left school; we had both been in the same form as Yaron (the world is so small!). Leesa said she had heard about my accident and wanted to visit me; I was extremely touched. We were in the midst of a catch-up when one of the nurses came in. She explained that because my room was so large, I would have to share it with another new patient. This nurse could see from my face how upset I was: I've never shared a room in my life, let alone with a stranger.

This nurse then left to discuss it with the other nurses. She then came back after a while to say I could actually go home as I lived so close; I just had to take a copy of my rehab timetable and come back for all my sessions. I jumped at the chance. My mum and nan thought I must've got it wrong when they arrived later, but Leesa confirmed they had said I could go home. I told Leesa she was my lucky charm. My mum then drove me home that afternoon. Though my family had come every day, and some friends had managed to squeeze a visit in, most people didn't even get the chance as I was an impatient for such a brief amount of time! As I saw Ryan at home every weekend, even he didn't come to the NRC. As he says, 'I've spent enough time in hospitals to last me a lifetime, thanks!'

From then on, Mum drove me in for my rehab sessions for a few hours a day Monday-Friday before picking me up afterwards. This only lasted for another month until November, as NHS input was gradually starting to wind down. By November, I then only had to come back for one hour once every week for 6 weeks for continuing physical rehab. This hour involved using equipment like the cross-trainer and throwing and catching bean bags. The point of this was to start trying to connect my brain with my physical movements again: wherever the bean bag was being thrown (e.g. on my left side, up high), my hands would have to move to that area of the room before the beanbag got there so I was ready to catch it.

During one weekday afternoon at the beginning of December 2015, Heidi practised my journey to work with me on public transport. I had suddenly gone from commuting to and from work twice a day in rush hour, to not getting on public transport at all for nearly half a year. I tried to be brave and I travelled to work on my own before Heidi met me at my work station to travel home with me. After I'd done it once, I wondered why I'd been worrying about doing it at all.

I was discharged from all NHS care completely in mid-December 2015. I had a couple of further follow-up calls with Sarah, but she was happy with my progress and then these also stopped. This is not uncommon: NHS care can only take you so far and you seem to be cut adrift and completely on your own once your NHS input stops. This is, however, by no means a criticism of the NHS. So many people were involved in my initial recovery that I can't even name them all: paramedics, nurses, consultants, doctors, physios... all the care and help I first received was exceptional. I would like to thank every member of the NHS who ever assisted me.

It was in mid-December 2015 that I had finally admitted to myself that I was nervous about going out completely on my own again. While I had practised my journey to work with Heidi earlier that month, I had no one at all to babysit me anymore now I'd been discharged. The last time I had been out completely alone was on 6th June 2015 (and look how well that ended!). I think it was nerve-wracking for my family the first time I went out completely on my own, but they knew I wanted to try and do things unsupervised as an adult again. I started with little

## "Everything is broken"

trips out shopping or meeting friends for dinner; although I was initially nervous about getting things like tubes and buses again, I simply made myself do it. Then it was after I'd done it once, I realised it was fine and I was worrying about nothing. My accident had been less than five minutes from my parents' house, and I always needed to walk past that turning wherever I was going. I had to force myself not to let this phase me: it seemed illogical to feel scared about something I can't even remember.

A side note: I wasn't allowed to drink around this time, and I guess I'm still not really supposed to now... It might have technically been classed as cheating, but it was around this time that I completed Dry January 2016. I'm not even really sure which charity Dry Jan is affiliated with, but I chose to raise money for the London Air Ambulance. I raised over £500 for them, which I was very happy with.

CHAPTER **6**

# The defendant

**"Everything is broken"**

t was around January 2016 that I really started to worry about the impending court case. I do not know much about the other driver, but I know he was 26 at the time (so only one year older than I). I do not wish to name him. He had been charged with 'causing serious injury by dangerous driving', and he had entered a 'not guilty' plea. His legal team was therefore doing the only thing that would've helped his situation: stating the crash was my fault.

I can't remember exactly when I was first visited by the police, but I remember having to give interviews about the day of the accident and the previous night. My liaison officer is called Craig; he was very kind and understanding. Craig told me that as the case was set to go to trial, my car was still being kept in the police compound in case they needed it for evidence later on. (I still remember his utterly exasperated expression when I asked if I could go and get my pink car mats back...) As well as taking a victim impact statement from me, Craig also took witness impact statements from my family.

I had passed my test in September 2014. I had then been in the, admittedly, very slow process of looking to buy a car, until Ryan bought me one five months later for Valentine's Day (I insisted on paying him back at least half the value, as I felt bad accepting such a huge present!). I was therefore a very inexperienced driver, and I had only been driving on my own from 14th February to 6th June 2015 when the accident happened. This is why I was initially very upset and wondered if I had unwittingly caused the crash. At this point, even the police reassured me that it was caused by the other driver. They said he was doing almost double the 30mph speed-limit.

I do understand that the other driver's lawyers were looking for anything to shift the blame back onto me: a lawyer's job is to defend their own client. They said I was not wearing glasses at the time of the accident. Doctors in the hospital confirmed this was correct, as they had taken out my disposable contacts when I had first been brought to A&E. I am in fact so blind I'd probably struggle to see the steering wheel without contacts or glasses.

I had been out the night before, but I'm not sure how they knew this (or maybe it was an assumption). I still remember shots of tequila had been brought to our table, but I had chickened out and run to the toilet to hide until they were all gone (as I knew I'd have to drive the next day, and I hate tequila anyway). The consultant who had been in charge when I was brought into A&E had confirmed that the level of alcohol in my system at the time of the accident was 0mg.

The police had also done their own speed tests along the road, so they had therefore been able to calculate an approximate speed the other driver was travelling at. They had worked out that he would've been driving between 50-60 mph, so by the time he'd braked, his car had collided with mine at approximately 30mph. Both cars were written off immediately. Added to the weight of the evidence the police already had, this all looked very promising and was definitely all in my favour. However, the 'not guilty' plea remained the same.

It was in approximately January 2016 that Craig had told me the case would still go to trial, but not until around August of that year. This would therefore give me over half a year to stew. I knew this would be immensely unhelpful. Since my NHS help had stopped in December 2015, I was now at a loss for what to do. As I have said before, I did feel a bit cut adrift once my NHS rehab had stopped: how could I possibly keep making improvements now? Or could I even improve any further at all on from this point? I thought it was absolutely futile worrying about a court case that I had no control over. However, I did have control over my physical and mental rehabilitation, so I decided I would take charge of that on my own.

Working at the Ombudsman meant I was entitled to free Bupa healthcare as part of my work benefits; I called Bupa to arrange some private physiotherapy in January 2016. I started weekly sessions with another muscular-skeletal physiotherapist called Suzy (who, like me, loves cats). I got a taxi to and from her clinic near my parents' house. I have no idea if this is common knowledge, but I personally had absolutely no idea that that I specifically required *neuro physiotherapy* rather than muscular-skeletal physiotherapy. In fact, I thought a physio was a physio: they all did the same thing! Although it still wasn't the exact type of physio I needed, I still found everything Suzy had me practice was beneficial for my physical movements.

At the same time, I had also joined the closest (and, more importantly, cheapest) gym near my parents' house; it is part of the chain simply called The Gym. I was now confident enough to get the bus here on my own (the bus stops at the exact point my car had ended up after the crash... how depressing!). Everyone laughs at me now, as I went from never doing any exercise since PE at school (which I didn't really participate in anyway) to suddenly becoming an overnight gym bunny. I didn't have the first clue about what to do, as I had never even been in a gym prior to this moment. I had used the one cross-trainer at NRC and I had found it ridiculously hard to do even 3 minutes at first. I started working with a personal trainer called Ali who showed me some of the other gym equipment I could use. I obviously lacked the core strength that most people my age should have, so as well as explaining that I hadn't got the vaguest idea about how to use a gym, I also had to explain what I could and could not do. Although he wasn't specifically trained in rehabilitation, Ali still made sure he tailored each exercise to my capabilities.

Looking back on it, I can't even remember a distinctive moment of marked improvement, but I seemed to suddenly realise one day that I was actually doing my bra up behind my back again...hooray! Yet still, my right arm would always flex at the elbow and bend up as I walked. I couldn't seem to help it; I would always have to remember to try and hold it down as I walked. Holding one arm down (so also keeping it still) likewise looked very bizarre. Therefore, the next challenge with my right arm would be concentrating on not physically holding it down and instead swinging it as I walked. After some weeks of serious concentration any time I walked anywhere, I suddenly realised my right arm would be swinging of its own accord as I walked.

Working with a PT and a physio definitely helped me progress with my physical movements; I continued seeing Ali and Suzy from January 2016 until the beginning of May 2016.

# CHAPTER 7

# Further rehab my lawyer organised

"Everything is broken"

So, from approximately January - May 2016, I tried my best to organise my own rehabilitation. Although this 'sort-of rehab' was not tailored to all of my specific needs, it was still better than sitting there doing nothing. I was still signed off sick from work at this point; my physical movements were still very laboured and slow. Many people also told me my voice had changed slightly (apparently it was slower).

As promised, I will now go back to what I touched on earlier. I explained that my parents had hired a lawyer, Kim Smerdon at Boyes Turner, to deal with my case. Mum and Dad had found Kim on the Headway website. I don't know what made my parents organise a lawyer for me at the time of my accident; even Dad says even he doesn't really know why they did it. They said they were just trying to find some sort of order through the chaos. They had driven to meet Kim in person just after my accident, and they had agreed to hire her. Dad said they were very impressed with Kim's professionalism and empathy. I don't think words will ever be enough to describe how grateful I am to Mum and Dad for involving Kim at this point. It is only because of this, and Kim's subsequent input, that I had the best possible recovery so far.

https://www.headway.org.uk/supporting-you/in-your-area/head-injury-solicitors-directory/south-east/boyes-turner/

## "Everything is broken"

After I had been discharged from hospital and I was back home, Dad had driven me to Kim's office to meet her face to face. Like my parents before me, I too was very impressed with her total professionalism. Whereas Dad had been dealing with all correspondences with Kim, we all agreed that I was now strong and able enough to be contacted directly instead.

Kim appointed Alex, from a company called Unite Professionals, as my rehabilitation case manager*. What on earth is a 'case manager?' I hear you ask (as I did too at the time). Alex was basically the co-ordinator of everything I needed to get back to who I was before the accident. As I have been told by many medical professionals, and read in many books, no two brain injuries are the same. The specific rehab I needed might not have been beneficial for another person, even if they had similar injuries to me. Alex therefore has to treat each case she deals with completely differently.

I first met Alex at my parents' house in February 2016; by around May, she had organised the three different types of private rehabilitation I needed:

1. Occupational therapy
2. Neuro physiotherapy
3. Personal training

Alex also arranged a pre-paid taxi account for me with a local branch so I could get to each appointment easily. I could now focus on intense, and specific, rehabilitation. (The legal team for the other side, even though their client was still stating 'not guilty', had initially agreed to fund 3 months-worth of private rehabilitation for me, but they did then go ahead and fund the whole lot over the course of over 6 months. I am very grateful for this, as they were not inclined to fund anything for me at this point.)

1.  **Occupational therapist (OT)**
    Seen from approximately May – December 2016

    *Occupational therapy provides support to people whose health prevents them doing the activities that matter to them.*

    *An occupational therapist can identify strengths and difficulties you may have in everyday life, such as dressing or getting to the shops, and will help you work out practical solutions. They can work with you to identify goals that can help you maintain, regain, or improve your independence by using different techniques, changing your environment, and using new equipment.*

    http://www.nhs.uk/conditions/occupational-therapy/Pages/introduction.aspx

The OT Alex organised for me is called Lucy; she was again instrumental to my recovery. As already mentioned, I had previously seen various NHS OTs from all the way back to when I'd just woken up; they had successfully started the long process of rehabilitation already. It was only once I was looking up a definition for an occupational therapist that I realised why, weeks ago, Jackie had let me practise applying my make-up: this was an activity that mattered to me.

Lucy was now in charge of private one-on-one OT, and I saw her once a week at home for two hours. Lucy created an upper limb home exercise programme for me, which included physical exercises, stretches and general tasks to complete. I've still got all of Lucy's emails, so I have been able to go back and read through everything again. Lucy would use some of her sessions to help me complete some tasks from this programme; these tasks ranged from anything to bicep curls with a small weight, to using tweezers to pick up paperclips. Repetition of these movements would help with both the strength in my right arm, and also smaller refined movements with my right hand. Lucy would also give me assignments to complete over the week before our next session (so essentially homework).

The improvements I saw with my right arm were by no means instantaneous. It was only by sticking to my exercise programme, and repeating each task over and over again, that I saw very gradual improvements over a long period of time; I realised how important it was to complete each activity with both intensity and repetition to see any sort of results. Even though lots of these exercises were quite monotonous, I still focused on completing them to the best of my abilities. It was only by rigidly sticking to my programme that I regained any sort of strength in my right arm and hand, which then in turn resulted in improvements with my handwriting, typing speed, and even texting (I had previously only used my left hand for this, but I started using my right hand too).

Lucy tailored her meetings so they focused on things that mattered personally to me. For instance, she gave me lots of activities to help with my handwriting, as I was upset it had diminished so much. Although I had previously been practising things like writing my name or the alphabet over and over again, this had become very tedious. Lucy gave me patterns to draw instead (for instance, a constant 'M' shape across the page). Copying these different patterns allowed my hand to almost re-learn the way of writing and how to hold a pen properly for ease of movement.

I think it's always better to focus on what I could do rather than what I couldn't do. Yes, practising handwriting patterns was monotonous and frustrating, but whenever I wanted to have a tantrum and give up, I would have to remind myself how much worse it could've been. I might have had to learn everything all over again starting from the letter 'A'. It is only thinking about things like that which would force me to 'get over myself' and just get on with it. It seems very boring to include, but I even had to practise cutting up a ball of plasticine with a knife and fork so I would then be able to use cutlery properly whilst eating a meal.

I still have issues with my short-term memory even now; Lucy would explain the areas she wanted me to practice before our next meeting and she would also print me off worksheets to I could tick everything off once a task was done. We could then look back over everything each week to track my improvements. For example, one day I might have to complete tasks from my programme, plus 20mins of typing practice. Lucy also added a column to remind me to complete the exercises the neuro-physio asked me to do at home too. I found it very helpful to see a physical mark of my progress. I have always been a visual thinker and I like to physically 'see' when I have done something; if anything, the TBI has only exacerbated this. On days where I didn't have to do something, Lucy then shaded in the relevant sections in black, just so I could see when I would or wouldn't have to do something.

Part of the work I did with Lucy involved talking through my executive function* and discussing how my brain injury had impacted on all areas of my cognition. We would then decide and practice strategies to help compensate for these difficulties; e.g. writing things down so I wouldn't forget them. Lucy would often set me tasks to complete in my own time, and then review and provide feedback on how I had completed it. For instance, I had to imagine one of my teammates at work was leaving, so I was in charge of planning their leaving present and send-off. Lucy went through my plan with me and I explained my reasoning for each decision I had made; I suppose it's a good thing I was always the organiser of such events for everyone at work anyway, so this exercise was an example of something I would definitely do in my everyday life.

Lucy often gave me photocopied tasks to do from *The Brain Injury Workbook: Exercises for Cognitive Rehabilitation*. Though she said I didn't need to, I then bought my own copy of this book. It is very long and has many practical exercises in it. I did find some of the tasks from this book quite difficult, which I was a bit sad about. But then on the flip side, I did find some activities so easy I skipped them altogether. Many of the specific exercises Lucy gave me focused on improving my flexible thinking, and my planning and problem-solving skills. These were the skills I would need when getting back to work.

This book also describes and explains how the brain-injured person could adjust to life after their injury. It also focuses on that person's loved ones, and how they might deal with such a situation. Brain-injured people can often lash out at those closest to them, so it is extremely hard to maintain romantic relationships or friendships during the recovery period. Many relationships break down completely, and friendships are often lost. It is an extremely eye-opening read, and it allows the brain-injured person to feel empathy towards the people closest to them (though I know in many cases, empathy is impossible for the brain-injured to feel). Depending on the part of the brain that is damaged, this can cause 'blunting'*, when a person's emotional responses are less intense than they should be. It can also cause complete changes in personality. TBI can cause a lot of aggression and anger, especially towards those closest to the sufferer.

Over the next few months, Lucy would consistently update my exercise programme as I improved, sometimes taking off some tasks completely. As I was due to move into a rental property with Ryan, Lucy also began working on strategies to help me regain a sense of independence. We used one of our sessions to cook a meal, as this was something I was a little reluctant to practise! (Remember when I previously said I hope I never have to cook a 'returned favour' meal for Sveta?) At uni, I had previously lived in student accommodation for three years and managed to survive without making anything beyond cheesy pasta, so cooking a real meal had never really been my thing at all… However, Lucy still encouraged me to practise this (I admit vital) everyday life skill. I did find chopping ingredients and standing up for a long time very tiring, but Lucy had definitely helped to show me that I could still cook a meal from scratch (if I ever wanted to!). Knowing how to make a meal is undeniably essential, so Lucy was definitely keen that I should practise some more cookery sessions. I've just always hated cooking though, so I really didn't want to at all… I have to give massive kudos to Lucy for coaxing me do even one session… She was definitely flogging a dead horse there!

It was around December 2016, after around 8 months, that Lucy discharged me from regular OT input. Lucy explained that sometimes people feel lost at this discharge point: whereas once they had to complete tasks to be looked over the next week, now I had no one checking if I had done anything at all. Lucy had arranged a follow up meeting for a few months' time, to check my progress and make sure I was still coping.

Ryan and I had successfully moved into our own rented flat in February 2017, which I thought was a great way of showing how life always has to progress forwards (despite any setbacks you might face). Lucy came to meet me in our new flat; she was very happy with my progress, especially as both she and I had been unsure how the stress of moving house might actually affect me. I had resumed having a 'normal' social life by now, and I had returned to working full time hours (including getting public transport independently to and from work). Lucy was then happy to discharge me completely. However, she made it clear I could email or call if I did need anything later on down the line.

Again, Lucy treated me with incredible kindness and empathy, as she specifically tailored each of her sessions around my goals. I had seen a variety of NHS occupational therapists throughout my rehab process. It was only once I needed help with absolutely everything that it opened my eyes to occupational therapy at all. In fact, it was only after I sat down to write this account that I realised just how many OTs I had actually had help from along the way: Sarah, Jackie, Heidi... The level of support and care I received from each OT I saw was essential to my recovery at every stage. I cannot thank them all enough for their assistance with everything that is important to me.

2. **Neuro-physiotherapist**
   Seen from approx. May 2016 – Jan 2017

   *Neuro physiotherapy is a specialist branch of the physiotherapy profession. Neuro-physiotherapists have specialist knowledge and skills in assessing, treating and managing a variety of neurological conditions. Neuro-physiotherapy differs from other branches of physiotherapy by acknowledging the many ways in which the brain can influence movement. Treatment is based on the latest research evidence and aims to address the person as a whole (mind and body).*

   https://www.neuro-physio.co.uk/helpful-questions-answers/what-is-neuro-physiotherapy/

By this point, I had of course now seen many OTs along the route of my recovery. I had also seen many muscular-skeletal physiotherapists, who had all helped me to improve my physical movements. However, I have to be honest and admit I didn't even know what on earth a neuro physiotherapist even was. As I've also admitted beforehand, I didn't even know there were different strands of physiotherapy at all! Though I suppose when you think about it, the very definition of neuro physiotherapy shows the brain controls everything we do, and it is indeed who we are as a whole. Once the brain is damaged, it has

## "Everything is broken"

a knock-on effect on every other aspect of the body, no matter how miniscule. How would (or could) neuro physio now assist with my own brain damage?

My neuro physio is called Helle, and she again loves cats (I have no idea how I kept finding fellow cat lovers!). Helle's clinic is near my parents' house; I got a pre-paid taxi there and back, and I saw her once a week for hourly sessions. Considering I didn't have the faintest idea what neuro physiotherapy even encompassed at first, I soon realised how incredibly helpful my sessions with Helle would be.

I was unbelievably lucky and somehow never suffered from any headaches (which seems miraculous considering the damage my brain had sustained). However, I would feel extremely dizzy if I turned my head too quickly whilst walking; I had originally just put up with this and tried to avoid turning my head at all when moving. This probably wasn't ideal, but I think I was just getting on with it at the time: who cared about some dizziness when my arm was still locked bent? This dizziness was caused because my vestibular system* had been damaged. So, imagine you'd just been spun around ten times, or had several shots in one go, and then you tried to walk in a straight line. That's the level of wooziness my brain would feel if I turned my head to the side too quickly.

To combat this, Helle performed the following two procedures:

1. Initially done to identify what I had: the Dix–Hallpike test*, which is a diagnostic used manoeuvre to identify BPPV (benign paroxysmal positional vertigo)*

2. Then the treatment for this: The Epley manoeuvre*.

But, I can almost hear you screaming, what on earth does all of that even mean!? I had to ask Helle to explain this whole procedure all over again to me, as even reading medical definitions didn't really tell me anything. Helle explained that 'crystals' had become trapped in the semi-circular canal of my balance system in my ear. The Dix–Hallpike test involves being moved to lie down quickly with a head movement to the side; this was to see if it brought on symptoms such as dizziness (which it did). These symptoms were then treated with the Epley (repositioning) manoeuvre to dislodge the crystals that had become trapped back to the correct place in my ear canal (so easing and eventually stopping my dizziness). The Epley manoeuvre involved more head movements whilst I was lying down; Helle compared it to one of those snow dome games where you have to move the snowflakes to a different place to settle.

Looking back at the report Helle wrote after first assessing me, I can see I had many other residual problems:

- Weakness around my hips
- Poor balance as soon as I shut my eyes, or tried to either keep my feet closer together, or stand on a soft surface (a foam balance pad)
- Inability to dual task. This meant I couldn't do things like walk and talk or turn my head while walking. I would lose my balance straight away.
- My walking was ataxic – i.e. unsteady and uncoordinated
- I couldn't keep my eyes fixed on something and move my head, or follow a target with my eyes, or look between two targets, without feeling weird.
- poor score on the Berg Balance Scale (BBS)*

All of the exercises I did with Helle then involved working on improving what had been identified above. Helle would time how long I could do many of the balance exercises for, so we could monitor my improvement over the weeks. We would also practice walking outside, moving my head, talking, walking over cobbles, and we even went around a supermarket. Each task was essential to improving the various weaknesses I had throughout my body. I have kept all the emails Helle sent me, so I have been able to go back through them all to see exactly what we worked on each week.

**"Everything is broken"**

This is a list of some of the rehab 'homework' Helle set for me to practise in my own time:

- Feet together, eyes closed. Aim to stand steady for 30 seconds
- Standing as still as possible first with eyes open, then closed on a foam pad (so you're on an unstable surface)
- Still standing on a foam pad and passing a small weight around your waist
- At the bottom of the stairs, right foot on the floor, left foot resting lightly on the step. Then swap.
- Walking in a straight line turning your head left then right
- Standing near a wall / cupboard / desk. Right foot stays still. Left foot steps in front then behind trying to stay within a narrow strip
- Heel to toe walking
- Clock - stepping around and weight shifting to random numbers as if standing at the centre of a clock face
- Stretching a yellow resistance band (the colours indicate how strong each band is) to work on right shoulder weakness
- Throwing or bouncing and then catching a tennis ball (for hand/ eye coordination)
- Carrying a cup of water while walking
- Exercises for further head/eye coordination – stick five playing cards to the wall with blue-tac; one in the middle, and the rest surrounding it up and down, left and right. Keep head still whilst looking at the middle card. Spend one minute moving only the eyes from the middle to the left card and back again. Repeat for each of the four cards surrounding the middle one.

Initially I found many of these exercises difficult, and I felt dizzy and unbalanced doing lots of them. After lots of practice though, I gradually started to improve. Helle would ask me to walk up and down the road outside her clinic whilst turning my head to look at her, which also definitely helped to improve my balance and wooziness.

Like an OT, Helle wanted me to get back to doing things that mattered to me. I remember we used one of our sessions so I could practice wearing heels for my birthday. I used to enjoy wearing 5-inch stilettos on nights out, but even now I still feel so wobbly in them. The whole point of wearing heels is to look elegant, so I felt like me hobbling along in them really ruined the glamour! So, I brought some heeled zip-up boots to a session, and Helle helped me practise walking in them instead. Once we'd gone across the room a few times, I felt a lot more comfortable: this heel size was a lot sturdier and far much more manageable!

Helle recommended other activities I could complete in my own time: visual saccades* and visual tracking games online. One game involved using my eyes to track a little figure running straight across the screen, and one involved a random picture appearing in different parts of the screen. I think these games were just generally extra work I could do to help with my eye movements and dizziness, and to help me work on my vestibulo-ocular reflexes (VOR)*.

As well as helping with my medical issues, Helle treated me with incredible kindness and empathy. Even when I was complaining about not being able to carry a hot drink without spilling it, Helle recommended a flask/mug with a lid instead; it is this compassion for every day 'little' problems that I found incredibly touching.

3. **Personal trainer**
   Seen from approx. May 2016 – Jan 2017)

Finally, I had quit my membership at The Gym near my house, and I now had a membership to Virgin Active funded instead. I also had funded personal training sessions, and I could get a pre-paid taxi there and back (though I would sometimes go to the little Tesco nearby for lunch, before getting the bus home instead). Theo was my new PT; he was not specifically trained in rehab, but he still tailored his instructions to my needs and didn't mind repeating things. As I have admitted, I had never been to the gym in my whole life before the accident. It was only now because I absolutely had to, that I'd ever been at all. I felt very stupid and frustrated every time I needed things to be explained or demonstrated again; Theo was very understanding about everything and he always showed me an exercise again if I wasn't sure about it. We also had some joint sessions with Helle, just so she could add her input on some of the exercises Theo was doing. They could then work together to create the most effective workout for me in order to maximise my recovery.

**"Everything is broken"**

As well as doing certain exercises and balance work, Theo also used to stretch out my muscles too (my current personal trainer does this now, so I have no excuse for not expecting the agony of it). I can't put into words how much this stretching out of the limbs hurts; it is only if you have experienced a PT doing it that you'll know what I mean. It simply feels like everything is on fire. It can't damage you unless it's done incorrectly, but I've been told this stretching even makes grown men wail like babies.

Although Theo ended up leaving Virgin Active, it was still helpful to work with someone who understood my needs; this helped me choose other PTs in the future. I think over the past 2 or 3 years, I've been a member of six different gyms and had six different personal trainers. Definitely making up for all the years I never went, then...

Occupational therapy, neuro physiotherapy and personal training all worked together to jointly improve my physical and mental wellbeing as a whole; I was now working with the right people to get me back to normal.

*Normal: the usual, typical, or expected state or condition*
https://en.oxforddictionaries.com/definition/normal

However, I have found the word 'normal' has become grossly unhelpful. What even is 'normal', and what did it even really mean anyway? Or what did this word even mean for me? I remember lots of my friends would always chastise me for complaining that I didn't feel 'normal' anymore. 'But you are normal!' was always shouted back at me. I personally think the definition of normality is entirely subjective, and that it is a very difficult concept to try and grasp when you really start to think about it. But, by this point, I was back laughing with friends (the usual), back always wearing black clothing (typical), and back enjoying the pub again (expected). So, I guess my chastising friends were, at least partially, right all along!

CHAPTER **8**

# Back to work

**"Everything is broken"**

went back to work at the Financial Ombudsman Service on 23 August 2016, about 14 months after I had the accident. My role was that of 'financial adjudicator', and I dealt with PPI complaints; I had started work there at the beginning of 2013. I appreciate all the help they gave me with regards to getting back to a normal working life.

As I had a year's worth of holiday to use from August-December, I booked every Monday and Wednesday off until the end of 2016. Going back to work on reduced hours therefore coincided with attending all of my different rehab sessions, so I would see Lucy on Monday and Helle on Wednesday. Lucy's help became particularly relevant at this stage, as we would talk through difficulties I had encountered at work, and we would work on strategies to overcome them. Rather than just telling me what I should have done differently in a situation, Lucy would always encourage me to think through an appropriate solution myself. At first no one was sure how I would cope with going back to work at all; people wondered if it would make me too exhausted. Luckily though, I had enough help to smoothly guide me through everything.

When I had still been off sick, I had been travelling into the office (I had of course initially had Heidi's help with using public transport) for just one hour once every couple of months. This was for meetings with a woman from HR called Rosie, and my new manager Rachel.

**"Everything is broken"**

Sarah's recommendations were taken into account, and we also had a conference call one day with Alex to make sure we were all working towards the same goal. Reading all of this back, I can see just how many names were involved in this process! Hopefully that will help readers understand the huge amount of people I was having discussions with about everything at this point... I had initially stated I did not want to go back to work before the trial was over and done with; but both Rosie and Rachel convinced me that it made no sense to stretch out the massive pause that had already been placed on my life.

I agreed and we eventually worked out a plan for a phased return within 12 weeks, gradually building my hours back to full time. I started on four hours for two days a week from late morning to mid-afternoon, so I missed the rush hour. This had then gradually built up to full time hours, but still only for three days a week. As mentioned beforehand, I had already practised the train journey to work, but I was still very nervous both about travelling in (and actually doing the work again). My balance was still very wobbly, and I was so out of practice with handling different cases. Rachel ensured a girl called Katie in my new team was made my 'buddy', and she would help me with everything.

I initially had two meetings with a company called Access to Work, a publicly funded employment support programme; they deal with reintegrating people back into the workplace after any sort of accident or illness. They could've provided me with any specialised equipment I needed, ranging from a smaller keyboard, to a different shaped mouse, or even a more supportive chair. It was very helpful to have such a vast amount of support available to me, but I have to admit that having so many names involved at this point was flustering me. I wanted to do things on my own and not have to answer to everyone and be babied; I didn't want to live like a child and have to ask to be 'allowed' to do things anymore. I confirmed by the end of the second meeting that I did not require any adaptations to my workstation, and I did not require any further input. That sounds ungrateful, but I don't mean it to be. I just needed clear goals to work for myself. Maybe the word 'I' is the keyword there: rehabilitation must focus around you. Anything you don't feel is working for you will ultimately be of no use: rehab is a highly personalised process. Only do what is right for you.

When I first got back onto my office floor, it felt like I'd never really left. The Financial Ombudsman Service is quite a large organisation and our offices are dotted around different floors and buildings. Menal had saved everything I had left on my desk the Friday before my accident, and she had kept it all in her locker for me. It only included useless stuff like pink pens and Kinder Egg toys, but I was still touched that she had been so thoughtful. It was lovely to see many of my old colleagues and my old managers Zoe and Mike again, but many of my workmates had already left. I was happy that at least some of my friends were still there, and we immediately feel back into the old routine of all scheduling lunch together (which I seemed to suddenly be in charge of again, so I don't know what they did when I wasn't there!).

We had a major reshuffle at work around the last few months of 2016, and Katie was no longer in my team to help me. I instead then got help from a guy called Pagey (his surname is Page, so he was always Pagey to us). Then at the beginning of 2017 all of the teams were mixed up again as people moved onto new workstreams. Rachel made sure I was still in her team, which I was very grateful for. Although I didn't know everyone, this new team also had two guys I had first started with years ago: Chima and Clayton. Chima initially helped me and looked over anything I was unsure of. No one ever made me feel like an idiot, so I am very grateful for all the help I received from my colleagues. After a few weeks, I had now grown in confidence and didn't feel compelled to get my work checked anymore. Chima still sat next to me to answer any questions I had. I found this especially helpful doing hour-long phone shifts, which involved speaking to anyone who called in about any issue.

Although Rachel and the guys obviously knew about my situation, I was unsure how to broach the subject to all the people in our new team. How could I casually explain being brain damaged? 'Hey everyone, so I had a brain injury (a traumatic one at that!) and then I had a year off sick to recover… but I'm just dandy now!' It was only after we'd been in the new team for a couple of months that I felt confident enough to tell a few people about my car accident and TBI. I remember my team-mates all being incredibly and visibly shocked. I don't really know what your 'typical brain injured' person should even look like. If anything, this gave a massive boost to my confidence. No one had noticed anything

**"Everything is broken"**

out of the ordinary, even about things I was worried about (such as my still laboured movements, or my speech¬). It made me truly realise how subtly I have changed. Sorry for another cliché, but it's made me appreciate that however someone looks on the outside, this will never tell you anything about what's going on inside. I had told everyone I was thinking about leaving work entirely to focus on writing a book, but I could only do this once my claim had been settled. This book had only ever been a fleeting idea before I got the feedback from my team: they all said it was such a fantastic idea. I guess it was at this point that I made up my mind. Although it would be difficult, I would definitely sit down to write this account.

I felt a great sense of achievement by not letting my accident dictate what I would do with my life. By January 2017, I was back to working full-time hours 5 days a week, and I had been discharged from all types of rehabilitation. I would like to thank everyone who was involved (you know who you are!) for ensuring it had all gone as smoothly as possible.

# CHAPTER 9

# The court case

**"Everything is broken"**

W hile all of this was happening, the court case was looming like a shadow in the background. To keep my mind off it, around mid-2016, Sveta had suggested that I should go to a SilverLining meeting. Sveta had previously come with me to a Headway meeting, and everyone there was a lot older than I was. SilverLining is a brain injury charity similar to Headway, but it specifically deals with younger people: everyone I met here seemed to be in or around their 20s like me.

**http://www.thesilverlining.org.uk**
*'In the UK, every 90 seconds someone is admitted to hospital with an acquired brain injury. Brain injuries have the potential to impact every aspect of life and, due to the complexities of the brain, every injury and recovery is unique.'*

Although I was quite reluctant to even go to a SilverLining meeting at first, Sveta yet again came with me for support. In this group, we went around the room in a circle and each member talked about the specific type of brain injury they had had, and the circumstances that had caused it. Even though our situations and injuries were so different, and no one else was even involved a road accident, I still found it comforting to speak to others in a similar situation to mine. I think going to this meeting was the moment in time where I truly realised that no two brain injuries are the same, and no two recoveries will be the same either. Everyone there had their own story about how they acquired their brain injury: some were born with theirs, some got it through illness, and some even simply hit their head in the wrong place after a fall. I found it almost morbidly fascinating how this injury can affect anyone from any walk of life, in such a huge variety of ways. I would like to thank Sveta for making me go to this meeting: it truly made me realise how lucky I have been. It even made me feel slightly guilty for whinging about my limited physical movement and my initially slurred speech. I could have easily suffered far worse injuries. If anything, I realised how little I truly had to complain about.

So, the SilverLining meeting did help distract me for a while, but I then couldn't help going back over and over the trial in my mind. I honestly had no idea about the legal side of my case: I thought there would be one trial and that was that. I don't know if this was me being naïve or just completely ignorant of how the legal world actually works. Luckily, nearly everyone at the Ombudsman had studied law, so they all told me that a case would be split into two: the criminal side and the civil side. The criminal side would only focus on whether or not the defendant would be found guilty of his charge: 'causing serious injury by dangerous driving'. Then, the civil side would be how much I could claim for the injuries I had suffered from. I feel like I drove my lawyer Kim slightly mad at this point asking her relentless questions, but she had to explain to me that she is not a criminal lawyer. All she could do was focus on the civil side of my claim: criminal and civil cases are completely separate entities, which was definitely news to me!

The trial was due to take place at the end of September 2016, so I would have been back at work for about a month by this point. Craig, my police liaison officer, had constantly reassured me not to worry, as the weight of evidence was all in my favour. The police had obtained footage from the scrap yard at the top of the road, which showed the other driver speeding. The police had also done their own speed tests down the road, so they knew approximately how fast the other driver was going; I had been wearing contact lenses, and I did not have any alcohol in my system at the time. In fact, Craig told me that even if I had been over the drink drive limit, it wouldn't have mattered. Either way, although the police would have had to address that issue at the trial, the other driver shouldn't have been going so fast.

Then one day at the beginning of September 2016, Craig called me completely out of the blue. He told me that the other driver had now changed his plea to 'guilty', so there now wouldn't be a criminal trial at all. I just remember sitting there in shock; I was so incredibly relieved that I didn't have to face him. What would I have even said? I remember absolutely nothing from that day, and I don't think I ever will remember anything either. As there was no trial because the defendant had changed his plea, there was only a sentencing in mid-October 2016. The judge sentenced him to 12 months, which he then appealed against. The next judge was satisfied with original sentence and did not change it. At last, the criminal side of things was now finally over.

HR and my manager had been right; I was so glad I didn't put off going back to work for so long. Craig had called to remind me that Velma was still being kept in the police compound, as she would have been needed for the trial, so I had to call them up and give the go-ahead for her to be crushed. I was so sad and felt like an even worse owner that day (and I never got my pink car mats back either...). As the criminal side was now finished, Craig said that he didn't need to contact me anymore: he and everyone else in the police had got me the justice they wanted for me. They had undeniably all done an excellent job, which I will always be grateful for.

So, now I had already 'won' the criminal case, the civil case and Kim's input could begin. However, Kim had already warned me that this process could take anything up to a year and a half.

From the end of October 2016 to about the end of March 2017, I had numerous meetings with a huge variety of medical experts, ranging from neurologists to psychologists, to neuro occupational therapists. They would all then write a report of their findings for Kim to add to her file. One of the doctors, Neil Brooks, was based in Milton Keynes, so Dad drove me to that meeting (Dr Brooks again had several cats, which I was very happy about). One of my other doctors was called Phil Mitchell; I told him I liked his name, and he then told me he also has a son called Ben. As an avid EastEnders fan, this brought me great joy. Although all these medical meetings could get extremely tedious, especially when I got tests wrong or found them difficult, it felt like I was always given some sort of light relief in each meeting, in some way or the other.

## "Everything is broken"

Another meeting that stands out was one Dad had to come to with me (as they needed a family member's point of view too). I was already upset about this meeting, as I accidentally dragged Dad to it a month early. I tried to cheer myself up by saying at least I got the day right, even if I was a month out... this doctor remarked that my voice was a bit 'flat', and it was lacking expression or intonation. I felt a bit sad about that, but then I discussed it with Dad and we agreed I was hardly going to be overtly expressive in a medical interview anyway...

I also saw medical experts from the defendant's side to ensure that we were all striving towards an accurate final report in the end. I think having a medical report from the defendant's side only added weight to my argument: everyone agreed that the car accident had caused me severe brain damage and will affect me in a variety of ways for life. I remember failing yet more basic cognitive tests for this doctor and feeling very down about it.

Then one day in May 2017, again completely out of the blue, Kim called me to say that the defendant's legal team had made an offer to settle my claim now. This was the second phone call to leave me sitting there completely speechless: we were only about 6 months into what should've been up to a year and a half's worth of reports and tests. I immediately questioned why and wondered if they were settling now because they didn't want me to be awarded a much more substantial amount in the end. Dad and I arranged a face-to-face meeting with Kim at her office later that week. She spent hours going through the whole offer, and she also got it checked by a barrister. Everyone was in agreement that it was a fair offer, and it looked unlikely that I would get any more in the end anyway. So, whereas everything had been so initially slow and dragged on for seemingly endless months, everything was suddenly happening within a matter of weeks in a totally unexpected whirlwind.

I spent about two weeks deciding if I wanted to accept the offer, which I eventually did. Soon after, work agreed to me taking a year-long career break. I promised my team-mates I would now use this time to focus on both writing this book, and further rehabilitation.

# Afterword

_____

Reading all of this back, it feels like I am talking about someone else. Apart from this accident, I have very rarely ever been to the doctor. I have never taken any medication for anything and, as I mentioned beforehand, I didn't need to take any after the accident. In fact, apart from the odd winter cold, I have seldom been ill at all. Since I was discharged from hospital completely, I haven't been back to the doctor for anything medical. I suppose I was probably overdue for some appointments when I had my accident, then.

I went back to my parents' house recently, and I saw the council have now altered the road markings where I had my accident. As it is such a wide road, they've had the space to move the whole turning slightly over to the left. This allows more room to see oncoming traffic, and vice versa. Probably a bit late for me, but I hope this will help stop any further accidents in the future.

As I studied English Literature at university, I understand how cathartic and freeing reading and writing can be; this was part of the reason I wanted to write everything down. I wanted to map and fill in the story of my recovery, so I could clearly see where I was beforehand compared to where I am now. Writing has helped alleviate the negativity I felt: once the words are on paper, they are no longer eating away at my mind. Reading anything from fiction to autobiographies as I have recovered has been a great outlet for any sort of pain I felt, from frustration, to anger, to sadness. I now want to put this accident behind me. I want to be able to turn something that was potentially devastating into something that could help others. If my account offers someone else even a sliver of hope after a traumatic brain injury, no matter how it occurred, then that is all I can ask for. I hope my account might even shed new light on the sheer complexity of sustaining and recovering from this kind of injury.

On Alex's recommendation, as I was writing this account, I read James Cracknell and his wife Beverley Turner's book, 'Touching Distance', about James' own recovery from a TBI. It is a very moving read, and I feel that it expertly showcases the vast differences of the TBI two people may suffer from. James explains that he became very aggressive and difficult post-accident, and almost seemed to morph into another person in front of his loved ones' eyes. A bit that really resonated with me was James explaining that he was convinced that red meant 'go' at a pedestrian crossing. I found this moment of utter confusion regarding an everyday activity, that even primary schoolchildren don't struggle with, extremely poignant. Even though I never experienced anything like that, I found I still had great empathy for this moment. It is impossible to describe what experiencing an injury to the mind feels like. If one imagines that left means right, up means down, green means stop and red means go, perhaps this will try to explain it. Nothing is as it was, and nothing makes sense anymore.

> *'The brain is a fascinating and mysterious beast.'*
>
> BEVERLEY TURNER

I've tried to write the most accurate account I can (warts and all). A lot of this book, especially the beginning, has relied on the memories of others. I try to stop myself thinking about the 'what ifs'. If I'd left the house 30, or 10, or maybe even 5, seconds earlier or later that day, then it's unlikely that any of this would have ever happened at all. I suppose in the grand scheme of things, I could've done a million things even slightly differently that day. Every time I catch myself thinking like that, I have to tell myself it's all negative stress, all counterproductive. I could spend the rest of my life wishing I'd done something even slightly differently that day, but what's the point? I have to accept what has happened.

'*Understanding is the first step to acceptance, and only with acceptance can there be recovery.*'

JK ROWLING

It took me a very long time to write this account; I kept accidentally repeating what I'd already written in different sections. I would often suddenly have some sort of brainwave and note something important down to include. I would then go back to my drafts and see I'd already included this idea the day before. It was also very hard to try and split everything up in a logical order. Whereas most stories will have a clear beginning, middle and end, I found that many aspects of my recovery overlapped and even integrated into each other. Reading this account back, it almost sounds like a film. It even sounds like I could've exaggerated my injuries, or even made some of them up. I honestly do not know why I have made what medical professionals would argue is a very good recovery, considering the severity of my injuries.

With regards to driving again, I spent a huge amount of time and money learning in the first place, so I didn't really want to allow it to be taken from me. I've completed tests with a doctor for the DVLA, and they have confirmed that I am still medically fit to drive. I've also completed driving assessments for a charity called Hertfordshire Action on Disability (HAD). They have thoroughly tested my physical and mental capacity to drive again post-accident: they agreed that there would be no harm in me getting a little automatic car for practising local journeys for now. I will then to go back to their test centre for one final assessment in the near future. I have since bought myself an auto Ford Fiesta. She is a G reg, so of course her name is Ginny. People have asked me if I'm scared of driving again, but I literally cannot remember even one solitary second of the day of my accident. I guess I can't fear what I have no recollections of.

I feel that it is only going through this experience that I have learned to appreciate the nuances between physical and mental strength, and how they depend on each other. It was only through having something taken away from me physically that I had to coax myself mentally into working on getting back what I'd lost. I'm not sure if that makes sense, so I'll provide an example. I found it so frustrating when I could just about walk painfully slowly from one side of a room to the other: this *frustration and exasperation* forced me into realising that it was only by physically *practising* walking around unaided that I would ever regain a smooth gait at all. Every time I wanted to get into bed and cry in defeat or complain that I'd never get back to the way I was before, I would tell myself that the only person who could help me was *me*. There is always a point in battling through the rehab process: even one small improvement is better than stagnating in the same, unchanged state. Baby steps.

Today, I have been left with on-going damage on my right-hand side:

- right dominant hemiparesis
- inability to 100% straighten the right arm – it has a permanent 'catch' if I straighten it quickly
- odd numb sensation if I chew on the right side of my mouth
- my right knee 'caves' (it bends inwards and it's slightly crooked)
- my right scapula 'wings' out slightly
- limited dexterity and handwriting with my right hand, plus a tightness/stiffness in movements
- slight imbalance in my posture (but no one who meets me now would notice it, it is only the people who knew me from before who can tell)
- it is hard to describe, but my right leg permanently aches now (it is just a dull kind of ache which is exacerbated if I do a lot of exercise)

I have also been left with the following:

- risk of another stroke (this decreases the more time passes since my accident)
- risk of developing epilepsy
- very mild aphasia (a condition that affects the brain and leads to problems using language correctly, which made writing this book a lot of fun...)

- reading in my head seems to be fine, but I have found that my reading aloud seems to be slower now (my brain cannot seem to translate the written word into speech as fast)
- can't run (no big deal as I never ran anywhere anyway) – I've now had to edit this, as I managed to run on the treadmill for the very first time in my life last week (with my new PT Sean making sure I didn't fly off the end or fall over!)
- can't wear high heels
- technically can't drink (but I may or may not ignore this at the weekends...)
- general weakness throughout my body, so I must keep going to the gym forever (great...)
- some cosmetic scarring (but apart from my tracheostomy scar, no one would ever see it)
- I find double clicking the mouse on a computer hard (which again made typing this a lot of fun...)
- terrible memory unless I've written it down somewhere (I can get quite upset if I forget about something, but I think this is a very hard thing to compare with how I was before. I think perhaps sometimes I can be very harsh on myself; I need to remember that everyone forgets things from time to time.)
- damaged eyesight (I now need a stronger prescription)

Although I am therefore by no means completely 'cured' now, I think that comparing the injuries I initially sustained to the above list will show how far I have come. I am glad this accident didn't happen during my education. If I had been at uni at this time, I know I would not be able to write lecture or seminar notes now; my memory might fail me, and my brain might not even be capable of processing new information anymore at all. But I've deliberately used the word 'might' here. I realise these are further 'what ifs' and further possibilities that might have happened.

But it is hard not to imagine even more 'what ifs' looking at that list: what if I get epilepsy, or what if my movement on my right side remains limited forever, or even gets worse? But, as I've learned from my accident, it is impossible to predict anything in life with 100% certainty. My accident was an utterly unpredictable, random event. But I'm afraid that's just life: you simply don't have the time to mope. Sorry if that

**"Everything is broken"**

sounds a little blunt or crass, but life goes on. Even after a totally earth-shattering event that affects every single aspect of your life, tomorrow will still arrive regardless.

I had heard that it takes up to 2 years to recover after a TBI. I have since spoken to other medical professionals who tell me it is actually 5 years. Either way, it's very difficult to try and put any sort of timescale on fully recovering from such a differentiating injury. How do we even define 'recovery', and what does it actually entail? How can you ever even recover from a 'broken brain' at all? Perhaps it is wrong to even use the word 'recover': the word should be 'adapt'. And surely even 'broken' isn't the right word at all anyway: it should be 'damaged'? What is 'normality' anyway, and who is in charge of measuring it? Something that is entirely 'normal' to you may be viewed as ridiculous or pointless by another person, regardless of whether or not they have sustained any sort of brain damage. Although we cannot see the injured brain, it is still a physical injury. But then how can you 'see' someone's personality? The brain would appear to be simultaneously physical and intangible at once. Surgeons can remove part of the skull and physically look at a brain, but there would be no difference in looking at my brain compared to your brain. They are all the same physical shape, colour and density: so, where do our personalities come from? Is that something separate altogether from the brain? Do we have a soul that inhabits another part of us?

Every time I've found rehab difficult or pointless or frustrating, I simply wanted to give up. It felt like everything I once was, and everything I'd once been, had been taken away from me. I felt like it was utterly futile trying to change at all: I just wanted to sit on the floor and wail. I think it definitely was meeting other people who had sustained far greater injuries and aftereffects than I that really brought it home how little I really had to complain about. Whenever I felt that rehab was meaningless, I simply forced myself to persevere. I know I am the only person who can change my quality of life; the emergency medics were only in charge of actually *saving* my life. *Living* it is all down to me.

I have never needed to rely on anyone else for anything in my adult life, so I don't see why this should stop now: I can't stand being pitied. It has been recommended that I continue to see medical experts at least once a year for the rest of my life... But I want to live a 'normal' existence and get back to my never needing to see a doctor for anything. It is medical opinion that I will need some sort of walking aid by 65, but I guess we'll just see about that in the future. Nothing in life is certain.

Writing this account and meeting other people at SilverLining and Headway has truly opened my eyes and shown me how lucky I am. I've found out that many people who have had brain injuries no longer have a sense of smell or taste. Many also have to learn to walk, talk, or write again; there are no two brain injuries which are the same. Depending on the area of the brain most damaged (front, back, left or right), this will always affect the symptoms suffered from, the subsequent recovery, and the long-lasting effects forever. I don't know why I've been dealt this hand, but I am just so grateful my senses were not damaged. The thought of not being able to smell my favourite perfume or taste my favourite food or drink ever again is horrendous. I almost can't even bear to think about how bad learning to read and write again would've been. Although I do still have short-term memory problems, my long-term memory seems to be fine. The thought of forgetting every person I've ever met, or every experience I've ever had in my life is unbearable.

I have become a bit fanatical about writing lists now; I think this has stemmed from problems I have had with my short-term memory loss. Whereas I was always a bit of a 'list writer' anyway, I do think I've moved up a gear with it now. I just feel that if I write something down (just as a text in my notes on my phone), I will not forget it. I like to also have tasks to complete the next day, no matter how seemingly insignificant. I then feel very calm once I have deleted everything from my note. These notes may even be as simple as 'gym, wash hair, writing'. I think friends have noticed me always double and triple checking times or venues when we meet up, but everyone just seems to humour me...

I understand why so many people hate the driver who hit me, especially as he tried to put the blame on me. However, I believe that personally harbouring any hostile feelings towards him will negatively impact me. No amount of feeling anger towards him, or feeling sorry for myself, will change what has already happened.

**"Everything is broken"**

*'What's done cannot be undone.'*

SHAKESPEARE MACBETH, ACT V, SC I -

It seems remarkable to me that I am no longer friends with many people I thought I'd always be connected to. However, I know the friends I have surrounding me now will always be there for me. Even people I had not seen for years made the effort to come to visit me in hospital. Why should I waste energy worrying about people not bothering anymore? It's easier all round to greet uninterest with silence.

As I said right at the beginning of this book, I hope that reading my account might provide some sort of hope for someone else who has been through any sort of TBI. If anyone else is in a similar situation where someone else is at fault, I hope my story has helped to showcase the importance of acquiring proper legal aid as soon as possible. It was only because Mum and Dad involved Kim from so early on that I have had the specific rehabilitation I needed. I had no idea what an occupational therapist or a neuro physiotherapist even were, let alone what they did, until Kim appointed Alex as my case manager to organise everything for me.

Conversely, I also understand that someone can acquire a TBI from something as everyday as falling over; no one else even has to be involved at all. TBI is not fussy about who it targets, or when or where it will strike. I have discovered that there is no such thing as 'the same' kind of TBI. No two people will ever experience exactly the same injury or aftereffects. Just as every person on the planet is an individual, a brain injury must be viewed in this way too. No matter how a TBI is sustained, it is vitally important that the *correct and specific* medical help and rehabilitation is organised (exactly around that person's needs) as soon as possible. I've found it's better to regret action rather than inaction. We could be feeling exhausted after the gym (action), or we could sit there and mope because our movement will never be the same (inaction).

In my opinion, the recovery I have made is thanks to the vast amounts of help and support I received (and continue to receive today) from everyone who is still around me. I have accepted that I will never be exactly the same person as I was before the accident, but I am trying my hardest to get back to as close to that as possible (although everyone who knew me from before the accident agrees that it seems crazy to think I'm a bit obsessed with going to the gym now!).

I believe a major reason I survived is because of the love, hope and support everyone gave, and continues to give, me. I keep a folder in my bedroom of every single 'Get Well Soon' card I ever received. This book is dedicated to my family, friends and partner. It is also dedicated to every medical or legal professional who assisted me in any way, however small. You have truly made all the difference.

May 2018

—

# Appendices

---

*'Hope never abandons you, you abandon it.'*

GEORGE WEINBERG

## Phil Stevens, March 2018:

Although this is about Jessica, it would be fair to say we are an unremarkable family. I am Phil, my wife is Sue and we have a son, Matthew and his older sister, Jessica. Most fathers have a special relationship with their daughters, but Matthew warned me about introducing Jessica to you, because it was likely to be an unrealistic, sugar-coated, Disney-heroine spectacular.

Sue and I are both strong-willed and fiery, so it should come as no surprise that Jessica carries one or two family characteristics with aplomb. Jessica can certainly slam doors shut with the best of them when angered. Jessica can also be stubborn and single minded when faced with challenges. However, depending on the circumstances this could be a benefit as you will see later. Jessica claims to be impatient which I have never noticed simply because that is a bit of a family trait too.

Jessica as a child had a gift for English. After graduating from Royal Holloway, University of London, she then decided to plough on with a Masters, also at Royal Holloway. Whilst at University, Jessica had a part time job at French Connection where she learnt about fashion and customers, becoming confident and articulate. She obtained an excellent job in Canary Wharf in a dedicated team offering financial support to the public, working with fellow graduates of a similar age. Friendships were formed and Jessica obtained the unlikely nickname of Jeff from North Wheezy (don't ask her why!).

Picture a beautiful sunny day in early June 2015, the first real summer day that year. My son Matt and I had gone to St Albans for lunch and a stroll in the countryside. Sue stayed at home because she wanted to see the Andy Murray tennis match. Jessica was driving to see her partner Ryan, a drive that she had completed several times before in her black Polo. In St Albans I was just parking the car when a call came in from Sue on my mobile phone. 'Come home immediately, Jessica has been involved in a car crash and has been taken to hospital in the London Air Ambulance.' I prayed she was still alive all the way home. Later we found out that she was turning right at the top of our road and was t-boned by a bigger car that had been driven round a blind bend at nearly 60 mph on a clearly signed 30 mph road.

Jessica had suffered multiple injuries including a broken pelvis, badly bruised ribs and shoulder, a collapsed lung and a traumatic brain injury (TBI). Her life had been saved at the roadside by a combination of the attending ambulance crew and the doctor from the Royal London Hospital who was with the Air Ambulance. Sue and I were driven to the hospital in a police interceptor unit as quickly as possible, to be able to say goodbye, as the police said she had been so badly injured. Fortunately, the brilliant Major Trauma Team and the Intensive Care Unit (ICU) at the Royal London Hospital worked their magic and she survived, albeit in a medically induced coma. Visiting a loved one in the ICU is a truly shattering experience. You feel so helpless because you can do nothing positive but simply be there, especially if the patient is unresponsive.

Being a busy ICU, the patients are in constant need of attention, meaning that a lot of our time at the hospital was spent in a bleak waiting room, with nothing to do. One of the first things an experienced ICU nurse told us was that with brain injuries she had seen tragedies and miracles in equal numbers and nobody could predict the likely outcome. Luckily, the neuro surgeon informed us that an operation on Jessica's brain was not needed as there had been no further bleeding in her brain. Days turned to weeks and there was nothing to do but support Jessica as best we could, given she was in a coma.

You think you know what the worst day in your life is but one day Sue and I were waiting outside the ward for the nurses to give the all clear so we could visit Jessica. Then the emergency alarm sounded from Jessica's bed and every nurse in the area rushed to her bedside carrying various items of emergency equipment, including the crash cart. Breath held, prayers sent up, and two minutes that felt like two hours. Then a nurse appeared, smiling. "Sorry you had to see that, but the nurse was changing the breathing tube and just needed an extra pair of hands."

We were told by the doctors and nurses that it may be beneficial to play music to Jessica and read her favourite poetry, which we all took turns to do, the only way I could ever play Beethoven to her. Her best friends kept her up to date with Towie and the latest gossip.

Then, after 18 days, a senior doctor in ICU called Sue, Ryan, Svetlana (one of Jessica's besties) and I to a meeting in a private room, bizarrely with a nurse who had never treated Jessica. He simply said, "There is no point talking to the neurologist, as he would only tell you what I am going to tell you." Why do professional people say that? Just knowing a neuro-surgeon doesn't make you one! He informed us that Jessica would **never** recover, would **never** work again and would **never** come home. I asked him whether it was a brain stem injury, and he said it wasn't but that "everything was broken," apparently with abnormal brain patterns.

To their credit, both Ryan and Svetlana said that they would never abandon Jessica and would do everything in their power to help her, whatever the outcome. In despair I spoke to the brain injury charity, Headway, and one of their counsellors said that after just 18 days nobody should predict such a bleak outcome based upon abnormal brain patterns. Then the following day one of the doctors from the Air Ambulance came to check up on Jessica and realising that Sue and I were feeling desperate, he informed us that ICU doctors were good at keeping patients alive but didn't understand the brain injury rehabilitation process. He added that it took some patients longer to process the anaesthetics out of their systems than others, but Jessica would become more aware as the days and weeks passed and may eventually come out of the coma. He also said that once Jessica was awake, the hard work for the family and loved ones was going to start. The doctor encouraged us to take heart and be strong for Jessica, (gold medal that man!).

After 5 weeks Jessica was transferred to a more local hospital, the Central Middlesex in Park Royal, where she was destined to make an incredible recovery with one particular morning etched forever in Sue's mind. Jessica was sitting up in bed with a big smile on her face and greeted her visitors by name as if she had just woken from a night's sleep.

Well, we didn't have the urge to celebrate as we all had to encourage Jessica to accept the way she now was and if she wanted her life back she would have to motivate herself and do everything the rehab specialists asked of her. Even though Jessica awoke with her long-term memory intact, she had to re-learn just about everything else we take for granted in life. Some of Jessica's achievements are: -

- The nurses put a mitt on Jessica's left hand to stop her pulling her feeding tube out which she spectacularly removed in 1-minute flat when the nurse turned her back

- When the nurses removed Jessica's tracheotomy tube, they said it may take 10 to 14 days to wean her off the breathing apparatus. They never had to replace it because Jessica was breathing unassisted very strongly

- She shrugged off a chest infection in 3 days whilst in the ICU

- When the neurologist visited with his entourage he politely asked Jessica how she felt and did she have a headache and she replied: "I have had worse hangovers"

- The same doctor mentioned that her parents both played badminton and asked if Jessica did too, to which she replied: "No, I am a source of continual disappointment to my family". Our Jessica was back!

- Jessica learned to put her lipstick on with her left hand within 3 days of waking up as her right hand was temporarily frozen

- She persuaded the doctors to take her to a hairdresser out of the hospital

- She was having a terrible time sleeping so the doctors allowed her home for a long weekend. She slept for 13 hours in her own bed – what a difference that made!

- The physiotherapists at Central Middlesex came up with a plan to get Jessica walking unaided within 14 days. It took her 10!

Jessica has recovered against all the odds and our eternal thanks go to some wonderful unsung heroes in the Royal London, Central Middlesex and Edgware Hospitals. If we were to gather those heroes in a room there would be 50 to 60 of you. The fabulous nursing staff all treated Jessica as if she were an awake patient and not in a coma and did everything they could to encourage and support her including noticing that she had beautiful teeth and brushing them twice a day. Also, the family's gratitude to all those who know Jessica, all her friends and her partner and the people who know Sue and I – thank you so much for your prayers, your kind thoughts and your support. It really did make a difference in our hour of need.

Our family, like many others, had no idea that the leading cause of mortality and disability amongst young adults is Traumatic Brain Injury. In 2013/14 there were 162,544 admissions to hospital for head injury (Headway website) or 4,445 every day or 1 every three minutes. According to Luke Griggs, Director of Communications at the Headway Charity,

> "Many of those admitted will face an arduous battle to rebuild their lives and relearn lost skills most of us take for granted, including walking and talking. Even those who make a good recovery are still likely to require some short-term support and information."

Whilst I do not have any medical training, the following ideas may help you:

- Organise a visiting rota

- Control the media output. Set up a closed user group for the sharing of information and progress reports – it will save making dozens of telephone calls whilst still staying in touch

- Keep a diary, noting any questions or advice you may need from the medical staff. Also note what the doctors say to you

- Contact your local Headway Charity group who can offer advice and support

- You will be under immense stress. If at any time you feel that you cannot carry on, make an appointment with your GP and discuss how you feel

- When transferring a patient to a local hospital nearer to where you live, research their facilities and ensure that the physiotherapy team knows how to deal with a TBI patient

- Keep up with your hobbies and sports – this will help you maintain your mental and core strength

- Be careful about reading too many articles on the internet. Each TBI case is different and you should discuss prognosis and treatment with the doctors at the hospital

- Try to be diplomatic and not fall out with medical staff, family and friends despite the stress you are feeling. They are trying to help

- When the rehabilitation starts you will need all your strength and resolve – eat regular meals and ensure that you support one another. The patient will need you to be strong and supportive to help them through a troubling time

*'One who gains strength by overcoming obstacles possesses the only strength which can overcome adversity.'*

ALBERT SCHWEITZER

## Judith Stewart, Head of Business Development and Client Relations at Unite Professionals Ltd, February 2018:

Alex Jones is one of Unite Professionals Ltd most senior and highly experienced brain injury Case Managers. Alex's role involved completing a holistic assessment of Jessica's needs and aspirations for her future. This was then guided by her regularly reviewing her treatment pathway and appointing the most appropriately qualified and experienced clinicians to ensure she facilitated the optimum outcome for Jess.

A Case Manager is someone with rehabilitation experience who is appointed to make clinically informed recommendations for treatment and services and to liaise with all the treating clinicians to co-ordinates these services.

Recounting their first meeting, Jessica remembers feeling very nervous about meeting another person and having to re-explain her frustrations and disabilities. At that time, she was only receiving 1 hour per week of face to face support via the NHS – this was simply not enough and Jessica broached this head on, venting her frustrations at progress and telling Alex, "I've got a list of what's wrong with me and if you can be the person who can provide treatment to make me feel better, I will be on board with working with you."

Alex has an infectious energy and can-do attitude and she immediately recognised the need for some clear client-centred goals to promote recovery, as prospects had been significantly narrowed over time for Jessica.

Jessica always took pride in her appearance and regularly used to straighten her own hair, a movement function she was unable to perform post-accident. This activity was introduced to improve strength, dexterity and co-ordination under the direction of an excellent Neuro OT to regain full movement over time.

Alex was accessible, knowledgeable, and able to answer any questions Jess may have. Jess was not interested in receiving lots of phone calls or letters, so together they agreed the most appropriate and preferred channel of communication. Meetings would be arranged in Jess's lunch hour as major fatigue would set in post-work.

Jessica's family reassuringly reflected that "Alex was invaluable as Jessica's professional Case Manager, because she relieved the pressure on us as a family in trying to organise the minefield of finding the right people to support Jess; it was all taken care of so efficiently and promptly with Alex on board."

Alex took time to address the family's needs and helped educate Jessica's parents around what had happened to her, why she needed support in cognitive, vocational and physical rehab and how they could contribute. Jess remarks that the shocked reaction to her progress from friends and family triggered a positive emotional reaction and she felt inspired to achieve even more.

Jessica started a graded return to work programme in the summer of 2016 with support from an appointed Vocational OT service researched by Alex and the team Unite Professionals. She was well monitored by her HR team and supportive co-workers. She routinely and independently continues to visit the gym following an increase in confidence and endurance.

Today, there is a renewed and inspired focus with Jessica taking some time out to write her rehab story. She invited Alex to learn more at a recent catch up. Jess demonstrated her progress, confidently problem solving the complex route change from her new home to the meeting venue totally independently. Alex reflects back to early meet-ups where Jess could not walk and talk at the same time as it was too much to process and her vestibular balance was really unstable as they mounted escalators. What a long way she has come.

In Alex words, 'Jessica is a remarkable, mature young lady, who is totally driven and an incredible human being. The injuries she sustained impacted every single area of the brain - you cannot get a more severe diagnosis. She has taken total control of her rehab journey and focus for her future life, and it has been my utmost honour to witness her strength of character to keep her goals central to optimise the best recovery possible. I will be buying a copy of her book when it hits Amazon!'

Unite Professionals Ltd, Case Management. Where "your rehabilitation is our priority".

*'Success is not final, failure is not fatal:*
*it is the courage to continue that counts.'*

## Ryan Young, April 2018:

On the day I nearly lost her, I'd been together with Jess for just over 6 months (but I'd actually known her for years by this point). I was heading over to my friend Rich's house – we were due to be staying the weekend to look after his cat, Jerry. This was something that Jess had no problem with, as she's always got time for a cat. As Jess was leaving, the last thing I'd hastily messaged her was (later regrettably) "bring charger" as I'd forgotten to pack mine. She replied with "k" – a classic sign that your girlfriend is not best pleased with you.

I arrived at the house in the early afternoon, parked up my car outside and let myself in with a key that had been left for us. The cat came to greet me shortly after. Being a hot summer's day, it didn't take me long to check the fridge for a drink. Inside I found a bottle of rosé labelled 'for Ryan', and four cans of Heineken labelled 'for Jess'. Hilarious, right? I cracked open a beer and sat outside in the garden and likely began scrolling through social media on my phone to kill time.

With the information available on Google Maps, I knew how long it would have taken Jess to arrive and that there was no traffic that could have delayed her. Once it was clear she was late, I gave her a call – no answer. No big deal, I thought. Having not driven to where we were due to be staying before, there's a good chance she might have got lost or something. As more time passed, I became increasingly concerned. I kept calling her periodically, always with no answer. Eventually, it went straight to voicemail.

At this point I was starting to get beyond concerned. Not because I thought something had happened to Jess, but more because with her phone seemingly being out of power – she'd have no Sat-Nav, and if she was lost, she'd probably really struggle. As more time passed I thought about driving out to look for her, but I kept telling myself she'd probably arrive at the empty house if I did so. Jess was hours late at this point. I simply kept attempting to call her phone, hoping that she'd have the good sense to stop somewhere and charge it so that she could call me for help.

I never got that call, and despite countless attempts, her phone never rang – until on one attempt it started ringing. But instead of hearing Jess answer, I heard her Dad's voice say my name. Had she gone all the way home to re-charge her phone, I thought? Her Dad promptly told me that she'd been involved in a serious car crash just outside the house and she'd been *air-lifted* to The Royal London hospital. S*** had most definitely just got real. I had no idea how severe her injuries were or the nature of the accident. Obviously if she had been air-lifted to hospital it had to be serious, but all the roads nearby her house are residential 30mph roads – this had to be more of a precaution, surely?

At this point my phone was very low on power. I didn't know how long I'd be at the hospital, but it would obviously be a long time – so I firstly headed back to where I was living to get my charger and then went straight to the hospital. I'd plugged in the hospital name into my phone's navigation app. From memory it was saying it would take somewhere between 1.5 to 2 hours to get there, mostly due to the typical London traffic. I had to go from outside west London into central. I didn't realise just how central until I was crawling past the Houses of Parliament and other landmarks.

I don't remember much else until it came to finally seeing Jess in the hospital. I was directed to an A&E area that was obviously designed for seriously injured people – almost like a basic intensive care unit. I didn't see her immediately – there were maybe about 10 beds in this area, all with curtains for privacy and the necessary monitoring equipment.

When I did eventually see Jess, it was definitely a shock. She was out cold, had a number of cables/tubes attached to her, and there were bloodstains on the floor. It didn't take long for someone to suggest I sat down because I'd gone pale as a ghost.

The doctors told us what they knew about her various injuries, the main one being a traumatic brain injury (TBI); Jess had been placed in an induced coma for some time in order to protect her brain. We waited around for more information for some time. Eventually they told us that they were going to attempt to reduce Jess's sedation to see how she responded. It was a pivotal moment. Had her brain injury been less severe she could have started to wake up and perhaps have been conversing with us soon after. Jess did not respond well to the reduction to her sedation and they advised this meant she would have to be transferred to a full blown intensive care unit (ICU). Any questions posed about whether she would be OK were answered uncertainly. It became clear that this meant Jess was going to be hospitalised for the foreseeable future. We wouldn't see so much as a semi-conscious version of Jess for weeks.

My coping mechanism emotionally was to avoid talking about it. Naturally people would ask about what happened and how Jess was, but as it wasn't good, I tried to avoid any conversation where possible. If I didn't have to talk about it, then I didn't have to think about it. Being something of an introvert this came naturally to me anyway. The emotions always creep up on you eventually though. The only person I would really open up to about it was my mum Karen. Usually I'd call her for a catch up while driving home when alone. She'd always reassure me that everything was going to be OK. Even though I knew she would say that regardless, it still helped. She'd often send me articles about 'miracle recoveries' from people who'd had similar TBIs too.

I did often send Jess WhatsApp messages at this time, as if in some way subconsciously communicating with her. I'd tell her that I missed her and that I was desperate for her to come back. I'd tell her about all the people that had been to visit her and other things that were going on. Each time I would message her on WhatsApp, her 'last seen' reading (showing the date & time minutes before her accident) never changed. There was no guarantee that it ever would.

Jess remained in an induced coma at the ICU – her injuries were numerous and the trauma her brain had sustained was severe. The purpose of the induced coma was essentially to rest her brain and give her the best chance at some kind of recovery but I'm sure there were a multitude of reasons for it. Jess was probably one of the longest staying occupants of the ICU at the time as the other patients in the room were wheeled in and out frequently, while Jess only left to have occasional operations or scans. The amount of cables and machines Jess was hooked up to had increased in the ICU. At one point she even had an operation to drill what was referred to as a 'bolt' into her skull above her right temple, which would monitor the constantly changing pressure in her head. During conversations with the ICU nurses they never suggested that Jess would be fine – only that it was possible for someone with her level of injuries to make *some* level of recovery. Being 25, age was on her side at least. You try to cling on to anything like that to stay optimistic.

Eventually though one day, seemingly out of the blue, a doctor called a meeting with all family members while we were visiting Jess. Jess's close friend Svetlana was there at the time, and she also came to the meeting room. The room was labelled 'family liaison' or similar above the door – immediately becoming apparent as the sort of place bad news gets broken to families as we'd never been taken into a private room to get an update on Jess before. The door was closed behind us. Once everyone was sat down, the doctor wasted little time getting to the point. He told us in no uncertain terms that at this stage they did not expect Jess to ever regain consciousness: the damage to her brain was very severe and probably irreversible. If she did regain consciousness, it was likely she would likely be in a permanent vegetative state. The news was brutal and devastating, shattering any optimism that we were clinging onto.

But even after this news, Jess's fate was never technically certain. The doctors had to give us the worst, which also happened to be the most likely, case scenario. We could only continue supporting Jess and being there for her always. Holding her hand, reading her books, playing her favourite music or simply talking at her were things we did to support her.

During downtime I would often read about TBIs on the internet. One thing I would definitely encourage anyone who is in a similar situation to be aware of is the 'Rancho Los Amigos Levels of Cognitive Functioning'.

Level I: No Response
Level II: Generalized Response
Level III: Localized Response
Level IV: Confused-agitated
Level V: Confused-inappropriate
Level VI: Confused-appropriate
Level VII: Automatic-appropriate
Level VIII: Purposeful-appropriate

http://www.traumaticbraininjury.com/symptoms-of-tbi/ranchos-los-amigos-scale/

This scale basically details what you can expect to see someone go through as their brain recovers from a TBI with surprising accuracy. While at this stage, Jess was still at Level 1 (no response), fortunately she did later to progress through the stages once she was weaned off her sedation. The Rancho scale helped me be aware of what behaviour I could expect from Jess as time went on, and even though some of this behaviour would be quite distressing, being prepared for it helped.

Around the time Jess had improved slightly, such that she would be classified as Level 2 on the Rancho scale, she was moved elsewhere in the hospital. At this point it was really a case of nurses looking after Jess and waiting to see how much further she would recover, if at all. Level 2 on the scale means 'Generalised Response - Person reacts inconsistently and not directly in response to stimuli'. This was exactly how Jess was. Her eyes were open and she would move her head, but there was no real consciousness there. Jess still had plenty of tubes attached to her, including feeding tubes going up her nose. She also strangely had her right arm locked in and pulled into her chest permanently. This could easily be the vegetative state the ICU doctor warned us about – it was a case of waiting and hoping for more progress.

Thankfully Jess did improve further, but the next few stages of recovery would prove the most challenging for everyone involved. Jess's new nurses always said there would be good and bad days from here on out – and they really were right. Jess was now transitioning into stage 3 – 'Localized Response: Person reacts inconsistently and directly to stimuli' – but the transition wasn't immediate. Some days she might look at you if you called her name, or squeeze your hand – some really encouraging signs. Other days she'd frustratingly seem to have regressed back to stage 2. It kept the fact that nothing was certain fresh in my mind. Eventually though, Jess obtained Stage 3 consistently. She was even starting to do cute things like (seemingly intentionally) reach out for my hand to hold. It was so relieving to see a semblance of her consciousness returning. Ostensibly things were on the up from here, but the next stage of recovery would be brutal.

Level 4 - Confused/Agitated: 'Person is extremely agitated and confused'. This one would be challenging for everyone, particularly the nurses. It was as though instinctual behaviour was kicking in, but Jess still had no idea what was going on or that she was in hospital. I can only describe this stage as *constantly* trying to deal with a mid-tantrum toddler manifested in the mind of your 25-year-old girlfriend. One of the first things Jess did during this stage was to reach up to her face with her left hand and swiftly pull out the (no doubt uncomfortable) feeding tubes going up her nose. She did this several times, and with her not being in a fit state to eat normally, she had to have her left hand wrapped in some kind of medical mitten so that she couldn't grab the tubes. The mitten had to be on really tight though, because given the chance Jess would pull the mitten off by biting it, then immediately pull out her feeding tubes again. Shortly after this the 'extreme agitation' set in. Jess would thrash wildly with her legs for hours. The kicking action would often spin her round in her bed, sometimes nearly pushing herself out. You had to be careful around the bed too as you could easily get kicked the stomach or face. It was particularly hard to see her like this. Getting to the next stage of the recovery couldn't come soon enough.

Once Jess had become less agitated and a bit more responsive, she would soon be moved to a new hospital which would focus on her long-term rehabilitation. Little did I know that I was about to have my first meaningful conversation with her in what seemed like forever. I was told one day suddenly that Jess was 'awake'. This was a huge improvement, but what did it really mean? I had no idea what to expect. Would her personality have changed? Would she even remember who I was? As I walked into the ward with Jess's parents the privacy curtain was drawn. Her parents waltzed straight through and cheerily said: "Hi Jess!". I was waiting behind the curtain apprehensively, until I was reassured enough to go through. Not only was Jess awake, but she was actually standing up! She was grasping onto some sort of frame which was obviously designed to support someone who was having difficulty walking – she was in the middle of a session with a therapist. Her hair was wild and shooting off in all directions – the ultimate bed head. She was responding to people talking to her, but she still seemed very dazed and confused. I said hello, but there wasn't any immediate connection. I guess she would have been mostly concentrating on trying to stay standing up. After the training session was finished, Jess was back in bed and her parents left for the café to give us some time alone. I immediately hugged her and she hugged me back – in my ear she simply said, "missed you". Although there was yet to be months of rehabilitation ahead of her (Jess would probably have been classified at about level 7/8 on the Rancho scale at this time), I knew from that moment I had got her back. We just had to pick up the pieces now.

# Glossary:

**Anticoagulants** - medicines that help prevent blood clots [administered to me through injections in the stomach]

**Ataxia** - neurological sign consisting of lack of voluntary coordination of muscle movements that includes gait abnormality.

**Atrophy** - gradual decline in effectiveness or vigour due to underuse or neglect.

**Blunting affect** - a person's emotional responses are less intense or as strong as they should be. A type of reduced affect, feelings and reactions are reduced in comparison to a normal response.

**Berg Balance Scale (BBS)** - widely used clinical test of a person's static and dynamic balance abilities.

**Bifrontal cerebral contusion** - a form of traumatic brain injury, a bruise of the brain tissue.

**BPPV (benign paroxysmal positional vertigo)** - causes brief episodes of mild to intense dizziness. It is a disorder arising from a problem in the inner ear. Symptoms are repeated, brief periods of vertigo with movement, that is, of a spinning sensation upon changes in the position of the head. Develops when calcium carbonate crystals, which are known as otoconia, shift into and become trapped within the semi-circular canals.

**Brain stem injury** - fatal health condition that can change one's memory, paralyse or change one's personality. The treatment required for brain stem injury is very expensive and causes serious life-long hardship to the family of the affected person, along with emotional and psychological problems.

**Case manager** - following an Immediate Needs Assessment report, a Case Manager will decide with the client on a plan of action, clearly stating what their goals for the future are. This could be anything from

referring you for further medical treatment with a specialist, to getting you some help around the house until you're feeling better.
https://www.uniteprofessionals.co.uk/frequently-asked-questions/

**Cerebral oedema** - a life-threatening condition that causes fluid to develop in the brain (brain swelling).

**Diffuse axonal injury (DAI)** - brain injury in which damage in the form of extensive lesions in white matter tracts occurs over a widespread area.

**Dix-Hallpike Test and Epley Manoeuvre** - used to test for and treat BPPV (specifically the most common form affecting the posterior semi-circular canal). Repositioning manoeuvre used to treat benign paroxysmal positional vertigo (BPPV) of the posterior or anterior canals.
https://entsho.com/dix-hallpike-epley/

**Executive function** - set of mental skills that help you get things done. These skills are controlled by an area of the brain called the frontal lobe.

Executive function helps you:
    Manage time
    Pay attention
    Switch focus
    Plan and organise
    Remember details
    Avoid saying or doing the wrong thing
    Do things based on your experience
    Multitask
    https://www.webmd.com/add-adhd/guide/executive-function#1

**Glasgow Coma Scale (GCS)** - provides a practical method for assessment of impairment of conscious level in response to defined stimuli (severe: GCS 8 or less)
http://www.glasgowcomascale.org/

**Haemopneumothorax** – combination of air and blood in the chest cavity.

**Hemiparesis** - weakness of one entire side of the body (hemi means "half").

**Intracranial pressure monitor** – a hollow screw ['bolt'] is inserted through a hole drilled in the skull. It is placed through the membrane that protects the brain and spinal cord.

**Mayo classification system** - provides a clear system for differentiating between mild versus moderate-severe TBI, which in turn guides rehabilitation

**Medically induced coma** - when a patient receives a controlled dose of an anaesthetic, typically Propofol, pentobarbital or thiopental, to cause a temporary coma or a deep state of unconsciousness. This type of coma is used to protect the brain from swelling by reducing the metabolic rate of brain tissue, as well as the cerebral blood flow. Throughout a medically induced coma, a patient's critical life functions are constantly monitored by an anaesthesiologist or other physician in a critical care setting only.

http://www.asahq.org/lifeline/anesthesia%20topics/medically%20 induced%20coma%20and%20sedation

**Polytrauma** - medical term describing the condition of a person who has been subjected to multiple traumatic injuries

**Saccade** - a quick, simultaneous movement of both eyes between two or more phases of fixation in the same direction.

**Severe brain injury** – usually defined as being a condition where the patient has been in an unconscious state for 6 hours or more, or a post-traumatic amnesia (PTA) of 24 hours or more. These patients are likely to be hospitalised and receive rehabilitation once the acute phase has passed. Depending on the length of time in coma, these patients tend to have more serious physical deficits.

A further category of very severe injury is defined by a period of unconsciousness of 48 hours or more, or a period of PTA of 7 days or

more. The longer the length of coma and PTA, the poorer will be the outcome. However, there are exceptions to this rule and, just as there is a small group of people who have a mild head injury who make a poor recovery, so there is a small group of individuals who have a severe or very severe injury who do exceptionally well.
https://www.headway.org.uk/

**Stroke** - the sudden death of brain cells due to lack of oxygen, caused by blockage of blood flow or rupture of an artery to the brain. Sudden loss of speech, weakness, or paralysis of one side of the body can be symptoms.

**Subarachnoid haemorrhage** - blood leaks into the space between two of the membranes that surround the brain. It is usually caused by a ruptured aneurysm. It can cause a stroke, and it is fatal in 50 percent of cases.

**Subdural haematoma** -a serious condition where blood collects between the skull and the surface of the brain.

**Tracheostomy** - an opening is created at the front of the neck so a tube can be inserted into the windpipe (trachea) to help you breathe.

**Traumatic brain injury (TBI)** - an external force injures the brain

**Vestibulo-ocular reflex (VOR)** - reflex eye movement that stabilises images on the retina during head movement by producing an eye movement in the direction opposite to head movement in order to preserve the target image on the centre of the visual field, or fovea.

**Vestibular system** - parts of the inner ear and brain that help control balance and eye movements. If the system is damaged by disease, aging, or injury, vestibular disorders can result in, and are often associated with, one or more of these symptoms, among others: vertigo and dizziness.

# Further information:

**Access to Work**
www.gov.uk/access-to-work

**Boyes Turner**
www.boyesturner.com
www.headway.org.uk/supporting-you/in-your-area/head-injury-
solicitors-directory/south-east/boyes-turner

*The Brain Injury Workbook: Exercises for Cognitive Rehabilitation*
www.amazon.co.uk/Brain-Injury-Workbook-Rehabilitation-
Speechmark/dp/0863889786

**Central Middlesex Hospital**
www.lnwh.nhs.uk/patients-visitors/locations-of-our-services/central-
middlesex-hospital

**Headway, the Brain Injury Association**
www.headway.org.uk

**London Air Ambulance**
www.londonsairambulance.co.uk

**Royal Free Neurological Rehabilitation Centre (NRC)**
www.royalfree.nhs.uk/services/services-a-z/neurosciences/
neurological-rehabilitation-centre-nrc

**The Royal London Hospital**
www.bartshealth.nhs.uk/the-royal-london
www.traumaticbraininjury.com

**Silverlining Brain Injury Charity**
www.thesilverlining.org.uk

*Touching Distance*, by James Cracknell and Beverley Turner
www.amazon.co.uk/Touching-Distance-Beverley-Turner/
dp/0099579685

**Unite Professionals**
www.uniteprofessionals.co.uk

*Where Is the Mango Princess?: A Journey Back From Brain Injury,* by
**Cathy Crimmins**
www.amazon.co.uk/Where-Mango-Princess-Journey-Injury-ebook/
dp/B00735HK4Y

www.traumaticbraininjury.com

www.neuroskills.com

# Acknowledgments and Thank You:

Simply saying 'thank you' will never being enough to express the gratitude and love I feel towards every person (and *pet*) who supported me throughout this time. The amount of people who visited me when I was still in hospital is staggering; you were all so strong for me. Thank you to everyone who helped me proofread sections of this book along the way, especially Lucy and Helle.

### Kim Smerdon (and everyone at **Boyes Turner**)
A special thank you to my lawyer Kim; your input has changed everything for me. You have given my life a level of security and stability that I never thought I was capable of achieving post-accident.
https://vimeo.com/tinkertaylor/review/234291187/f64fca514d

### My family –
Mum, Dad, Nan, Matt, *Chloe & Munchie*
Without your consistent love, support and hospital visits, I can safely say I would not have made this recovery. Thank you to Mum and Dad for organising proper legal aid when you did; without this help, the situation would've rapidly deteriorated. Lastly, thank you for the best housewarming gift of all time: my Maine Coon kitten Max! (I don't think I quite had enough cats in my life beforehand...)

Uncle Michael, Paola, Nina, James and Leo
Thank you for making so many trips from the other side of London to visit me in various hospitals: your visits always made my days easier. Thanks for bringing Sara to see me; she is a doctor who predicted I'd make a full recovery. And thanks again to Uncle Michael and James for painting the rooms in my new house - it all looks fabulous!

Thank you all for everything; I love you all and we got through it together.

### Ryan (and Karen, Craig, Emilia, Ali, *Bonnie & Bailey*)
I couldn't have wished for a better partner. Our 'yay, I didn't die!' road trip in a Mustang across America was the best holiday of my life. Thank you for being so relentlessly strong for both of us. Thank you for always being there for me throughout everything, especially when I'm being horrible/difficult/moody (see, I admitted it!).

*'I love you with so much of my heart that none is left to protest.'*
Much Ado About Nothing, Shakespeare, Act IV, Sc i

Karen, I'm so glad you knew how devastated I would've been if I'd woken up with a shaved head, so thank you once again for brushing my hair out for me!

Thank you to your whole family for always providing me with endless love, kindness and support.

**Claire** (and Laura, Jo, Nigel, Shaun and *Harley*)
Claire: as much as you've told me you couldn't live without my friendship, I couldn't live without yours either. You're my sister from another mister, and you will always be the Ted to my Tony; I will love you forever.

Jo used to work in Edgware hospital, so special thank you to her for always making the time to visit me after work!

**Claire and Laura - married on 28 March 2016** - I was Claire's only bridesmaid at her wedding; I was still in the midst of rehab at this point. Me, Claire and Jo all had our makeup and hair done before we all travelled to the venue in mint green camper vans. Claire's little brother Shaun (who will always be a new-born in my mind, despite the fact he was 18 at the time) helped me to go down the aisle, as I was still quite wobbly at the time. Then later on at the meal, I did a speech. I had complained to anyone who would listen that I didn't want to do one, as I was nervous about stammering. No one listened and I was bullied me into it anyway. Naturally, I included a joke about how I obviously didn't die on purpose because otherwise Claire would've had no bridesmaids. Perhaps a little dark, but I don't think Claire would've expected anything less.

**Mikael and Sofia - married 2 April 2016** – This wedding took place exactly one weekend after Claire and Laura's wedding, so it was still in the midst of my rehab. I think these two weddings are prime examples of life going on. I didn't have time to sit around moping when two couples had the most important days of their lives coming up!

Mikael was one of my workmates at the Ombudsman, until he selfishly left. Sofia is Mikael's beautiful wife, who looked stunning on her wedding day.

Menal and I went to get our hair and makeup done together in the morning beforehand, and it was such a beautiful day. It was so lovely spending the day with all my workmates on much happier terms, rather than them sitting around my hospital bed.

### The Coven
**Jess, aka Twinny/Serena** (and Diane, Malcolm, *Rosie & Sadie*)
Thank you for assisting with all my beauty projects on so many different occasions, from painting nails to half-heads of highlights! And for making my parents a USB stick (how old school!) of photos of (fridge appropriate) memories we shared together at uni.

**Svetlana** (and her name-twin mum Svetlana, Vlad and Alex)
Thank you for coming with me to Headway and SilverLining meetings; I never would have gone alone, and these meetings were so helpful. Though you may live in another country now, no amount of distance can break our friendship.

### Emma
Thank you for coming to visit me every Tuesday evening (on your only day off!) for weeks without fail; I always looked forward to it. I would once more like to apologise for once vomiting my terrible hospital dinner up all over myself and my bed right in front of you! What a spectacular treat.

Thank you all for your endless support throughout the darkest of times; you are the embodiment of what it means to be a best friend. I love you all. Thank you once again for surprising me with tickets to see The Lion King musical together, and thanks for a fab day at the polo!

### Wagg
Thank you for all your hospital visits, and for our infamous Nando's/'Spoons date nights after I was discharged! Thanks for all my apt gifts, especially my 'angry swearing cats' adult colouring book...

## Cigdem

We're been friends since Year 7, so I guess you're well and truly stuck with me now! One day I will buy us both unicorns.

## Deega

'I dare you to eat that yoghurt...' 'YOU THINK I WON'T?' The memories we have are priceless: from our holiday to Ibiza, to arguing with random men on trains... I'm so glad I met you in French Connection (when I was hungover every Sunday without fail).

## Joella and Alyson

You guys were the best housemates for my first two years at uni! You both selfishly then left me to do your years abroad, but we are proof that separation didn't change our friendship. You are my favourite badger (fadger?) ladies.

## Menal and Shumona

From painting ornaments, to complaining, to EastEnders, to afternoon tea, to farm animals (but only the cute ones) – I'm so glad I met you guys and we shared a work team, at least once upon a time! I will always be your Jeffrey.

Shumona – I still miss our weekly GBK visits! You're my favourite 'situational dresser'. This is why I'm sure it was you who bought me my pink sheep pyjamas when I was in hospital... bed-bound = pyjamas! But you don't remember if it actually was you... so I guess we'll never know now.

Menal – 'Jess, I'm picking you up and then we'll get our hair and faces done before Mikael's wedding.' Well, who am I to argue with that? Still so grateful to you and Mikael for organising a huge work group visit to see me back when I was in hospital. Loved my massive pink basket full of presents!! (And yes, the family cats immediately stole said basket to sleep in, the second I took it home.).

## Ray

Thank you for coming to see me every Tuesday afternoon on your only day off! (Not sure why Tuesday was such a popular day off...) Thanks for always bringing me sweets, debaucherous stories, and taking me on trips outside or to all the different hospital cafés in my wheelchair. Your pub will always be the best pub ever. Ever.

### Rich, Stevie & Jerry

I do hope Jerry has managed to eventually forgive me and Ryan for being such terrible cat-sitters! Rich, it's just so typical of you to get a new girlfriend after my accident. I've no doubt Stevie would have visited me in hospital too if you had only started dating just a few months earlier! Thanks for bringing me endless amounts of sweets in hospital, and thanks for occupying my parents for ages talking about football...

### Everyone who has helped guide my recovery

Alex, Unite Professionals – thank you for being the driving force behind organising all the different types of specific rehabilitation I needed. Your wholehearted empathy, compassion and organisational skills are unmatched.

Craig H (and everyone else in the police who worked on my case), Heidi, Helle, Jackie, Judith S, Lucy, Sarah E, Tania, Theo.

If I haven't remembered your name here, please don't think you were any less important to my recovery. Thank you to every member of medical staff who assisted me along the way:

- everyone on board the Air Ambulance the day of my accident
- every staff member who helped me in:
- the Royal London
- Central Middlesex
- Edgware NRC

### My old uni mates:

Andy, Annie, Ben G, Emma S, Jade, Jamie, Helen, Monty, Miles, Lizzi, Stuart

### My old workmates:

French Connection
Aleksandra, Arvinda, Fran, Kailee, Tara

**The Financial Ombudsman Service**
I've never seen a bigger 'Get Well Soon' card! (I'm ignoring the fact that most of you have left, so you technically don't fit in this category anymore...) To everyone who came to see me in hospital: I will never forget the levels of kindness and support you all showed me.

Ben D, Jake, James, Karl, Liv, Mo, Rishi, Zara

Adeena, Alison, Arjona, Charline, Chima, Clayton, Dami, Darren, Elaine, Gemma, Hirra, Jackie P, Jonny, Kainat, Katie F, Katie M, Kayleigh, Kunal, Maddy, Manny, Marta, Mike, Minal, Mollika, Mufta, Natasha H, Natasha O, Ngozi, Nik, Nimi, Matt, Paul, Pagey, Penny, Philana, Rachel, Rosie, Rossy, Sean B, Shalah, Tom, Yasmin, Zoe, anyone else I accidentally missed from (the now defunct) Y200

**Various other friends and people from all walks of my life (who didn't fit into one neat category)**
Ali, Aundre, Bharti, Carl and *Millie*, Catherine, Charlene, Tom and *Tilly & Gizmo*, Deanna, Lucy and Jonathan, Diana, Dina, Fleet Taxis, Gemma D, Hagger, Becky and *Pudding*, Hilary and James, Jenny, Judith F, Karen W, Leesa, Len, Easter, Rory and Kiara, Lila and Luke, Maureen and family, NCP staff who work with my dad, Patrick and Daisy, Ricky, Sarah V, Sean M, Shakiah, Sophie, Speller and Lucy, Suzy, T and finally, Yaron.